SMALLVILLE

SEASON 1

THE OFFICIAL COMPANION

Superman created by Jerry Siegel and Joe Shuster

SMALLVILLE: THE OFFICIAL COMPANION SEASON 1
1 84023 795 3

Published by
Titan Books
A division of
Titan Publishing Group Ltd
144 Southwark St
London
SE1 0UP

First edition September 2004
10 9 8 7 6 5 4 3 2 1

Visit our websites:
www.titanbooks.com
www.dccomics.com

Did you enjoy this book? We love to hear from our readers.
Please e-mail us at: **readerfeedback@titanemail.com**
or write to Reader Feedback at the above address.

To subscribe to our regular newsletter for up-to-the-minute news, great offers and competitions, email: **titan-news@titanemail.com**

A CIP catalogue record for this title is available from the British Library.

Printed and bound in Great Britain by MPG, Cornwall.

SMALLVILLE

SEASON 1

THE OFFICIAL COMPANION

Paul Simpson

TITAN BOOKS

ACKNOWLEDGEMENTS

Thanks are due to many people for their help in preparing this book. First and foremost, all those who so graciously gave up their limited free time to be interviewed on and off set; Kendra Crowther in Vancouver and Lisa Rose in L.A. for coordination above and beyond the call of duty; the Anglo-American Alliance (Katrina Gerhard, Jerry Boyaijan, Jenn Fletcher, John Mosby, Kerry Glover and Jill Sherwin) for the visual material; the Sophie Brigade (John & Val, Joe & Kate, Andy & Sarah, Clare, Cherry, Peter and Anali) for helping to free my time; Helen Grimmett for helping turn hours of interviews into practical material; Mark Warshaw, Nick Setchfield, Jayne Dearsley, Platform P.R., Luke Pulfer, Rod Edgar, Chris Golden and David Hughes for research material; Dad, Jenn and Ali for riding to the rescue at exactly the right moment; Katherine for support and inspiration in the final stages; Craig Byrne for all his help on and off the Web; Jo Boylett for her editing skills; and to Adam Newell at Titan and Chris Cerasi at DC Comics who made sure we all kept the faith.

Special thanks to Alfred Gough and Miles Millar for thinking of this new beginning and being available to discuss it despite the many other calls on their time — and to Jerry Siegel and Joe Shuster, without whom there would be no end to the story...
— Paul Simpson

The publishers would like to thank the following people who contributed to the *Torch* and *Ledger* articles featured in this book: Jake Black, Angela Dai'Re, Christopher Freyer, Lisa Gregorian, Karen Miller, Gena Murph, Will Rogers, Mimi Soo and Kathryn Zoucha. The publishers would also like to thank Phyllis Hume, Steve Korté and Sandy Resnick at DC Comics, and the entire production team of *Smallville* for all their help with this project.

DEDICATION
Dedicated to Sophie, my own strange visitor from another planet.

Welcome to SMALLVILLE KANSAS POP. 45,001 The Meteor Capital of the World!

CONTENTS

FOREWORD

You probably didn't know that the person responsible for creating *Smallville* was Arnold Schwarzenegger. Yes, that's right, the Governor of California. Remember his movie *Eraser*? It's the one with Vanessa Williams and that ridiculously big gun. Well, back in the summer of 2000 we'd just written a pilot for a TV series based on the movie. It was a high-octane piece, full of big budget set pieces and macho heroics. Having cut our teeth working for Joel Silver, it was the sort of project we could write with our hands nail-gunned behind our backs.

Below: Miles Millar.

It was developed under an overall deal we had at Warner Bros. Television. The script was tight and we thought it had a good shot if we found the right actor. We sold it to ABC and were looking forward to producing the pilot. But making a pilot is a little like unsafe sex — it's fun until the show gets picked up. Come on, would you want to spend five years of your life figuring out ways to "erase" people?

Anyway, the upside was that while we were scrambling to find someone to fill Arnie's oversized shoes (we looked at everybody from Ving Rhames to Patrick Swayze!) Peter Roth, the President of Warner Bros. TV, called and said he liked *Eraser* so much he wanted us to develop a second pilot. Our minds raced — what lame-ass action movie does he want us to rip off now? Then he told us the idea — "Superman in high school." We looked at the speakerphone, then at each other. Wow. Cool.

Considering that we had never written a script featuring teenagers, and neither of us had grown up reading comic books, it was a true leap of faith. So the irony is that if we'd never written *Eraser*, we would never have gotten *Smallville*. So, thanks Arnie, we owe you one.

When we first started working on the pilot, we said to ourselves that if this show didn't work we would abandon TV and concentrate on writing movies. It was liberating because we had nothing to lose. If we went down, we were going to go fighting. We haven't stopped fighting since. Of course, we didn't go into battle alone. We want to take this chance to thank some of the unsung heroes who have been in the trenches alongside us.

Above: Alfred Gough.

Litvack (nobody calls him John) — the true wizard behind the curtain. Steve P. — for always staying at our end of the tank even when the sharks were closing in. Jenette and Paul — for giving us DC's crown jewel. Len and Andrew — for helping us create this incredible world. "Crazy" Joe Davola — for manning the front lines in the early days. Chris and Shelly — for all those Friday night brainstorming sessions. Mike and Brian — for being smart enough to leave us alone. Andy Ackerman — for that lunch at the "Smoke House", you know which one. Bernard, Doug, Graham, David — for making *Smallville* come to life. Rob M. — the last man standing, your dedication has been a rock. Greg B. — for your friendship, vision and insane, caffeine-induced enthusiasm. Ken H. — for just being you. DeeDee, Coreen, Kathleen — for finding our spectacular cast. Dana and Matt — for putting up with us. Rene — for being the Jewish mother we never had. Greg Mc. and David L. — for allowing us to put our feature career on hold. Michael G. — for your mega-counsel advice. And, of course, to the fans of the series — thanks for not letting us get complacent. Your passion and wisdom is a constant source of inspiration.

Finally, we'd like to dedicate this book to Jerry and Joe — for creating one of the most enduring and inspiring characters of modern times. The world is in your debt, guys. ■

Alfred Gough & Miles Millar
Los Angeles, February 2004

GENESIS

"The challenge of *Smallville* was, how do we recreate this mythology in a way that is credible to a modern and youthful audience? How do we update a familiar theme in a way that makes sense?"
— Peter Roth, President, Warner Bros. Television

For over sixty-five years, one man has symbolized truth, justice and the American way. His exploits have been chronicled in comic books and on radio, in film and on television — even, in the mid-Sixties, on the Broadway stage. He is probably one of the most instantly recognizable people on the face of the planet. He is an alien, and his birth name is Kal-El, but his name on Earth is Clark Kent. He is better known, however, as Superman. *Smallville* tells the story of his formative years.

Superman was created by two teenagers not much older than Clark, Lana, Chloe and Pete in the hit TV series. Canadian Joe Shuster's family had moved to Cleveland when he was nine, where he became friends with Jerry Siegel, and they worked together on the school newspaper, *The Glenville Torch* (sound familiar?). In 1932, around their eighteenth birthdays, they published their own magazine: *Science Fiction, The Advance Guard of Future Civilization*. Although their pulp fiction only lasted six issues, issue 3 saw their tale 'The Reign of the Superman' see print.

This Superman was a very different person from Clark Kent's *alter ego*. He had superpowers, true enough, but they were given to him by a bald-headed mad scientist, and he used them for evil. He didn't reappear, but the idea of a Superman took root in Siegel and Shuster's heads, and in the summer of 1934, they reinvented the character as a hero. He now wore the familiar blue bodysuit, with red boots and the red cape, with a red and yellow 'S' on a shield on his chest — a cruder version of the stylized 'S' that has since come to symbolize the Kryptonian.

Siegel and Shuster tried to sell Superman as a newspaper strip without any success, but their sample work was forwarded on to Vin Sullivan, the editor of a new magazine, *Action Comics*. Sullivan loved the character, and Superman débuted in *Action Comics* #1 in April 1938. Nine months later, his adventures also started to appear as a newspaper strip. In February 1940, Superman's radio adventures began, and a mere three months before America was drawn into World War II, the hero bounded onto the big screen with the first cartoon from Fleischer Studios.

The mainstays of the story appeared very early: Lois Lane and Superman's secret identity as reporter Clark Kent were there from the very first issue of *Action Comics*, and issue 23 introduced a scientist, Lex Luthor (who, after a few appearances with red hair, would always be drawn bald). Clark's home world was originally simply described as a "distant planet", but became known as Krypton in the newspaper strip. Kryptonite itself was introduced in the radio show as K-Metal, before transferring to the comic books in 1949. In 1944, readers met Superboy for the first time. This was the teenage Clark Kent, having adventures in his home town of Smallville while still in high school.

In 1986, Superman's origin was retold by writer and artist John Byrne, excising much of the baggage that had grown around the character in the previous fifty years. Although this version of Superman, whose adventures continue today in numerous titles from DC Comics, developed his powers during his teens, he didn't don the red and blue costume until he went to Metropolis. The Clark Kent who grew up in Smallville had to learn to deal with his powers, while keeping them secret from his friends…

Every generation has had its screen Superman. Whether he's played by Kirk Alyn in the chapter plays from the Forties, George Reeves in the Fifties TV series, Christopher Reeve in the movies from the late Seventies and Eighties, or Dean Cain in the Nineties' series *Lois & Clark*, Jerry Siegel and Joe Shuster's creation has inspired audiences around the world for decades. In 2000, the world's first twenty-first century small screen Superman began to come into being.

Originally, film and television production company Tollin/Robbins Productions came up with the concept of a show about a young Bruce Wayne, before he became Batman. They took the idea to Peter Roth, President of Warner Bros. Television, hoping that he would be able to help them negotiate the rights for a TV series. "That was thwarted from happening," Roth recalls. "The feature division has a stake in the Batman character, and decided to put into development a feature film featuring the next incarnation of Batman. The feature division didn't want to compete with the television division, and suggested that we not be able to move forward with our television version. I was unable to help loosen that restriction, but around June 2000, Tollin/Robbins approached me again and said, 'What about a young Superman?' I thought it was a brilliant idea."

Roth had wanted to bring the adventures of Superman to the screen for over twenty years. "I began my career in children's programming at ABC," he explains, "and one of

Above: Where it all began: the cover of *Action Comics #1.*

A 6 PART MINI-SERIES BY BYRNE & GIORDANO

SPECIAL COLLECTOR'S EDITION! NO.1

THE MAN OF STEEL

75¢
CAN $1 00
UK 40c

THE LEGEND BEGINS

Above: A new beginning as John Byrne unveils a revamped Superman in 1986.

the properties I had the opportunity to work with was [the animated series] *Superfriends*, which of course included Superman. When I got into prime time in 1979, I was given the chance to develop something which I was particularly passionate about, and I tried my damnedest to develop a series targeted toward Sunday nights at 7pm for ABC which featured the teenage version of Superman. Unfortunately, the Salkinds, who had then just produced the very successful feature film, had every intention of doing a sequel, so I was thwarted as I couldn't get the rights from DC Comics."

Roth therefore was delighted with the chance to help bring a version of Superboy to the screen, as was Tollin/Robbins' Senior Vice President of Television Development, Chris Castallo. "It was always my dream to do something in terms of a property through DC, and Peter was very enthusiastic about the project," Castallo recalls. "He helped us navigate through the clearance situations."

"We then went about the task of marrying the right writers to the project," Roth continues. "We decided to go with Al Gough and Miles Millar, who are the developers of the property. I think of them as the creators of the show, although of course that title goes to Siegel and Shuster, the original creators of Superman."

Miles Millar takes up the story: "I guess it all started with a phone call from Peter Roth. We had a two-year overall deal here at Warner Bros., and Peter called us up and asked us to come in. It was his dream to do Superboy as a TV series, and we said that we liked the idea of doing something with Superman, but we didn't like the idea of the cape or him flying around." At that point, *Smallville's* motto 'No Flights, No Tights' was born. It goes right to the heart of the reinvention of the story that Gough and Millar created. "*Lois & Clark* had only ended four years earlier," Millar says, "and we wondered how we could make something that was fresh and new."

The idea that they came up with involved, Millar continues, "stripping him down to his bare essence, in a way. We wanted to lose the suit and see his humanity. We wanted to get inside his head and see the reasons he became Superman. What were the events that led him to decide that he was going to devote his life to saving people and making mankind better?"

Gough and Millar had met at the University of Southern California film school. Millar had come over from his native England on a program at USC, and the two men hit it off. In their last term at film school, they sold a script to New Line Cinema, which gave them the chance to become professional writers. In the seven years before *Smallville* began, they had written for both film and television, contributing to the story on *Lethal Weapon 4* and scripting *Shanghai Noon*, as well as being on the writing staff of the TV series *Martial Law* and *The Strip*, where they had worked with Peter Roth.

None of the creative personnel involved was interested in writing what Tollin/Robbins' President of Television Joe Davola calls "a soft show. We didn't want something that was just 'Truth, justice and the American way'." "There were two things out there in the zeitgeist," Chris Castallo points out. "*Buffy the Vampire Slayer* had really changed TV for young people, and showed how you could update mythology. And *7th Heaven* was still building its audience in its fifth and sixth years. We sat down and talked about

Above: Clark Kent in the cornfields.

how you get some of that Middle American iconographic family sensibility, that a show like *7th Heaven* has, into a show that has action in it. How do you take that tone and apply it to an action franchise? From the comic book side, we talked about the big criticism of Superman — that he's a big boy scout. He doesn't come from a place of darkness like Bruce Wayne does. If there was a subtitle for this show, it would be 'The Trials and Tribulations of Clark Kent'."

"This character has been in a thousand comic books, in radio shows, three TV series, numerous cartoon series — what could we bring out that was fresh?" Miles Millar asks. "When we started researching the project, we realized that his teenage years were a part of his life that had not really been explored." Al Gough agrees: "You see him when he crashes, and then once as a teenager in the movie, then he's in Metropolis. You don't know anything about those years, which was great for us."

GENESIS

Above: Lana Lang, complete with meteor rock necklace.

Although Chris Castallo at Tollin/Robbins is a great comic book fan, neither Gough nor Millar was. "When I started reading the research and learned that he had a girlfriend called Lana Lang, that was total news to me," Millar admits. "We have an appreciation of the years of talent, effort, and storytelling that's gone into these properties, but we bring a totally fresh, unbiased view of these things. We can take the pieces we like, and rearrange them and reinvent them. We're not labored or encumbered with remembering being six years old and falling in love with issue #19!"

"We're respectful of the source material, without being slavish to it," Gough adds. "It was also good that there's been so many different versions of Superman. He can be reinterpreted for different decades. In the Fifties he was a G-man, in the Eighties and Nineties he was a yuppie. In the first movie, he was a very lovable guy."

Though Gough and Millar were enthused by the clean canvas that writing about Clark's teen years in Smallville gave them, they still needed to find the hook that would enable them to turn the idea into a TV show that could viably create the hundred or more episodes needed for a successful series. "What's the franchise?" Millar recalls them discussing. "That's when we came up with the idea of the meteor shower. That worked for us in two ways. Clark Kent is superhuman, so each week we wanted him to battle superhuman things. So kryptonite landed on Earth and started mutations. We also figured that in this day and age, if a spaceship crash-landed in the middle of Kansas, within twenty minutes there would be thousands of people — media, CIA, NASA, FBI — just swarming on the place. The meteor shower could act as a camouflage as well."

"The thing that caused Al and Miles to be hired and was the basis of our first year was that notion," Peter Roth says firmly. "The kryptonite meteors were embedded in the meteor shower, ironically killing Lana Lang's parents, ironically causing Lex Luthor to lose his hair, ironically giving life to Clark Kent on Earth as others died. It created an entirely new emotional spin. How ironic that the woman Clark was most in love with lost her parents as a result of his arrival! And Lex Luthor's inexorable journey to the dark side begins as a ten-year-old redheaded kid who loses all his hair as a result of this meteor strike."

"If Al and Miles hadn't figured this out, the show would never have worked," Chris Castallo agrees. "As Al and Miles often say, ever since the franchise began in comics in 1938, it has been based on Clark Kent saving people close to him. If you're going to do a show about Clark saving people close to him a hundred times, you've got to have a device which puts those people in danger.

"Also, they have managed to bring Lex Luthor to town," Castallo continues. "It's a corny idea from Golden Age 1950s Superman comics, but they managed to get Lex into this town and into the lives of these teenagers in a very real-world sort of way. Lex never really existed within the DC Comics mythology in Smallville other than in that time period. But now, even if you step back and wonder what this older guy is doing with these kids, it doesn't feel weird. Al and Miles created a reality and a tone within the show that because Lex is such a worldly person and so empty inside, he's reaching out."

For their new version of Clark Kent's teenage years, Millar and Gough created new characters. Closest to Clark is Chloe Sullivan, the editor of the school paper, the *Torch*, for which Clark occasionally writes. "We wanted to see Clark as a boy reporter," Millar explains. "We wanted to know how Clark's interest in journalism first sprouted. We also needed someone who was an outsider who could actually say, 'You know what? Some really weird stuff happens in this town.' Chloe had recently moved from Metropolis, so had an outsider's point of view. Everyone else was blind to it, or ignored it."

Millar admits that the increased role of the other major new *Smallville* character, Lionel Luthor, was "a happy accident. He was in the pilot, and we kept using him in the first season. We always knew this, but it became clear that the show really offers an experiment in extreme parenting. Lionel provides a parallel with the Kents: Lex has this unbelievably twisted relationship with his father, and Clark actually has a very deep and emotional relationship with his parents."

"I'll never *ever* forget the day Al and Miles pitched their updated conceit for the

Above: Lex Luthor, newcomer to Smallville.

show," Peter Roth maintains. "I knew then and there we had something very special. The second highlight for me was the day we struck a deal with the WB. Another network wanted the show, but we finally struck a deal with the WB, which at the time was a landmark deal for the WB and for Warner Bros. Television. I felt a real sense of accomplishment that day."

Once they had the green light from the network and the studio, Millar and Gough had to work simultaneously on preparing the script for shooting and casting the series. "We've always been big fans of David Nutter's work," Millar says of the pilot's director. "He's the preeminent pilot director."

"He just seemed like the right fit," Al Gough adds. "He'd also done *The X-Files*, and he works very well with teenagers and green actors. He was able to set the tone, mood, and look. He came into the process just as we were about to start writing the script, and he came up with the idea for the final scene, where Clark is looking out and Lana comes up and dances with him in his dream. He said, 'You want to end with the guy and the girl — that's your series.'"

The producers were aware that the show *had* to be successful. "That was made clear to us from the very beginning," Miles Millar says. "Casting is the key for any television show. In a film, you can get by if you make a mistake by cutting somebody out. With a television show, you have to live with them for a hundred hours, so you can make no mistakes. We had the luxury of casting in October. Unlike most shows, which pick up in January and you've got four weeks along with every other show to do your casting, we had more like five months. We had casting reps all over America and Canada looking for Clark, Lana and Lex."

At one stage, the producers considered casting real teenagers in the roles, but decided that "in the proud tradition of *Grease* and *Beverly Hills 90210*, the kids are twentysomethings playing high school kids. It's a conceit that everybody just seems to buy," Al Gough notes.

The producers had intended to cast Clark first, but were blown away by the tape of Kristin Kreuk's audition for Lana. "Normally you take three or four people to the network, but we just said, 'She's the one,' and the network loved her. There's a haunted quality to her performance that's very touching." Tom Welling followed in short order as Clark Kent. "We put him with Kristin at the network, and they just had great chemistry," Gough recalls.

Michael Rosenbaum, however, followed sometime later. "We always wanted to get a comedian," Millar notes, "because they always have an innate need to please and be loved at the same time. Michael came into the room and basically took it over. It suddenly went from the part that nobody could agree on, to us finding the guy."

Former *Dukes of Hazzard* star John Schneider fit the producers' hopes for Jonathan Kent. "We wanted to have a recognizable face on the show," Millar explains. "And the baggage he brought was good," Gough adds. "*The Dukes of Hazzard* was a very rural show, so you could believe this guy had grown up running a farm.

"Initially we cast Cynthia Ettinger as Martha, but it was one of those cases where the actor and the role were not right for each other. All of us, including her, realized this during the process of shooting," Gough continues, "and when we cast about again, Annette O'Toole's name came up. She'd done the television series *The Huntress*, and for the fans she'd played Lana Lang in *Superman III*."

Allison Mack joined the cast based partly on her "rare ability to deliver large chunks of expositionary dialogue conversationally. That's a skill actors either have or they don't," Gough notes. "Pete was the hardest one to cast. We saw Sam Jones III on the Sunday before we started filming. He had a natural sweetness." That's something the producers were looking for in all their cast members. "The difference between a movie star and a TV star is that for five years you're going to invite these people into your life once a week, so they need a real sweetness, and I think all our cast do," Millar says.

The series is shot in Vancouver, Canada. "We looked at Australia," Al Gough reveals, "but in Vancouver we found a sort of Middle America landscape. We could find the barn and the farm, and Vancouver itself can be Metropolis. Also, quite frankly, from a production point of view, at the time it made financial sense to shoot in Vancouver because we could put more money onscreen, and they are in the same time zone as Los Angeles."

With cast and crew in place, filming on the pilot began in March 2001... ▪

Above: Clark, Lana and Lex look to the future.

THE EPISODES

October 1989: life in the small Kansas town of Smallville is changed forever by a devastating meteor shower. Three-year-old Lana Lang's parents die in front of her. Ten-year-old Lex Luthor loses his hair after being caught in a meteor's impact. And childless couple Jonathan and Martha Kent discover a young boy wandering away from the wreckage of a spaceship that has crashed amongst the meteors...

SEASON 1 REGULAR CAST:

Tom Welling (Clark Kent)

Kristin Kreuk (Lana Lang)

Michael Rosenbaum (Lex Luthor)

John Schneider (Jonathan Kent)

Annette O'Toole (Martha Kent)

Allison Mack (Chloe Sullivan)

Sam Jones III (Pete Ross)

Eric Johnson (Whitney Fordman)

THE PILOT

WRITTEN BY: Alfred Gough
& Miles Millar
DIRECTED BY: David Nutter

GUEST STARS: John Glover (Lionel Luthor), Adrian McMorran (Jeremy Creek), Sarah-Jane Redmond (Nell Potter), Malkolm Alburquenque (Young Clark), Matthew Munn (Young Lex)

Twelve years later: Clark Kent is now a teenager with some unusual powers. He is faster and stronger than anyone else his age. Clark's best friends at Smallville High are his boyhood pal Pete Ross and the school paper's editor, Chloe Sullivan, who has moved to Smallville from Metropolis. Chloe is continually fascinated by the many bizarre events that surround the small town as a result of the 1989 meteor shower. Clark is in love with Lana Lang, who is dating school football star Whitney Fordman, but can't get near her because she wears a necklace containing a green meteor fragment.

The new head of the local fertilizer factory, Lex Luthor, accidentally drives off a bridge, hitting Clark at sixty-five miles-per-hour. But Clark survives, and rescues Lex. As a result, Jonathan tells Clark the truth about his alien origins. The meteor storm also affected Jeremy Creek, a Smallville High student who was the 1989 scarecrow — a football team hazing tradition which involves tying a fellow student up in a cornfield, like a scarecrow. Finally recovering from a coma in 2001, he has developed strange electrical powers, and uses them to take revenge on those who hung him in the cornfield. Clark is made the 2001 scarecrow by Whitney, but is eventually rescued by Lex. Clark then stops Jeremy from attacking the homecoming dance.

JONATHAN: Sweetheart, we can't keep him. What are we going to tell people, "We found him out in a field"?
MARTHA: We didn't find him. He found us.

"I don't believe in doing shows for certain audiences," pilot director David Nutter maintains. "You have to reach out to every audience. You have to make it intelligent. You have to make it fun. You have to make it smart. And you have to respect your audience."

By anyone's definition, the pilot of *Smallville* fulfills all those requirements. It had a great deal to achieve. It had to introduce all the characters. It had to tell the story of Clark and the meteor rocks' arrivals on Earth, and the consequences for Lex, Lana and the citizens of Smallville. And, not least, it had to tell its own self-contained story. "David brought a scope to this that you rarely see in television," executive producer Al Gough notes.

Preparations for the pilot took some considerable time. While the producers and director were going through the casting process, they were also scouting for locations, and assembling a crew who could bring their ideas to life. "They had a very clear and

Opposite: Clark wonders how he survived the fall into the river.

Smallville Ledger

* * * Volume 62, Number 42 * * *

MOGUL'S SON MIRACULOUSLY SURVIVES CRASH

A small crowd gathered at the Loeb Bridge on Friday afternoon after word got out that businessman Lionel Luthor's son Lex had crashed his Porsche through the barrier and plunged into the Elbow River.

Reconstructing the accident, police speculate that a truck crossing the bridge earlier may have somehow lost part of its cargo. A roll of barbed wire was found near the scene, and Luthor's shredded tires support that theory. Apparently, the force of the blowout caused Luthor to swerve off the road. "Lucky for Lex it didn't happen three miles back, where the old stone wall would have taken good care of him forever," commented Officer Cub Johannsen.

However, Johannsen and the other responding authorities were at a loss to explain how the roof of Luthor's Porsche became peeled back like a sardine can, considering the guard rail was only waist high, and the car did not flip over before it went off the bridge.

By Sunny L. Kaye

deliberate vision," Tollin/Robbins' President of Television Joe Davola recalls. "I was up there [in Vancouver] making sure their vision was carried out. A lot of the design of Smallville was from Miles — a non-American's view of what America is."

As construction coordinator Rob Maier — one of the very few members of the Smallville team who worked on the show throughout its first two years — adds, "We were looking for the epitome of 'Smalltown, USA'. That was the essence of finding Smallville — it had to be cleaner than clean, nicer than nice, more beautiful than it would be in the real world. All of the people in Smallville are beautiful; all of the colors are bright and sharp." The other locations were also carefully chosen. "David really had a vision for the Kent family farm," Al Gough says. "It had to have an old world sensibility and tone," Nutter explains.

Some of that world was created digitally. With the exception of the scenes at the Kent farm, very little of the corn seen in the pilot actually existed. "We had grown ten thousand stalks of corn in a greenhouse that didn't grow more than two feet," Miles Millar remembers. For scenes such as Clark in the cornfield at the end of the episode, corn was specially flown in from Arizona, but the majority of it was created by the effects team. "There was only a foot or two of corn on either side of young Lex running through the field," Nutter recalls.

Australian production designer Bernard Hides worked wonders on the episode. For the scene in the graveyard between Clark and Lana, "he had to create a world out of

Above: Clark tries to come to terms with the news his father gave him.

nothing," Al Gough says. "There was a field and three trees." For David Nutter, "this was the scene that sells the show to me." Executive producer Miles Millar adds, "We tested this scene with an audience of both boys and girls, and boys would usually tune out of a scene like this, but they were totally into it."

"What's really magical about this script and this story is that Al and Miles were able to let the audience in on the hearts of these characters and what they were feeling," David Nutter says. "If an audience can emotionally care and be in contact with these characters, then you've got them. This is a perfect example of that."

CLARK: What are you trying to tell me, Dad? That I'm from another planet? And I suppose you stashed my spaceship in the attic?
JONATHAN: Actually, it's in the storm cellar.

In order to shoot the pilot in the sixteen days of main unit filming allotted, Nutter relied heavily on the 150 pages of storyboards prepared by artist Adrien Van Viersen, which allowed some scenes to be shot over a period of several days. "The porch scene was filmed in three different locations," Eric Johnson recalls. "The wide shot was at the farm, my close-up was underneath the football stadium, and Kristin's close-up was in the studio — spread out over the four weeks of shooting."

Warner Bros.' President of Television, Peter Roth, remembers watching the pilot at the House of Blues in Los Angeles, with "about 150 excited people who were watching it for the first time. The next day we were shrieking with delight when we got the numbers. It was clear we had something very special." ∎

DID YOU KNOW?

The interior of the Luthor mansion was filmed at Shannon Mews in Vancouver, which had also appeared in the pilot for *Dark Angel*, as well as in the motion picture *Along Came a Spider*.

METAMORPHOSIS

WRITTEN BY: Alfred Gough
& Miles Millar
DIRECTED BY: Michael Watkins
& Philip Sgriccia

GUEST STARS: Chad E. Donella (Greg Arkin),
Gabrielle Rose (Greg's Mother)

Lana is stalked by nerdy Greg Arkin, who becomes infected by meteor rock-affected bugs. As he begins turning into an insect, he kills his mother, then attacks Whitney in his truck. Clark rescues Whitney, and then he, Pete, and Chloe find Mrs Arkin's body. Greg attacks Clark and Jonathan, but runs away once Clark proves indefatigable. Whitney is unable to prevent Greg from kidnapping Lana, and Clark tracks him down to the old foundry, which is peppered with meteor rocks. Although he is weakened by the rocks, Clark is able to battle Greg, who inadvertently lets a mining scoop fall on him, causing him to split into little bugs, which escape.

Lex gives Lana enough clues to enable her to ask Whitney whether he was involved with scarecrowing Clark. Whitney admits that he was, and that he has lost her necklace, which Lex picked up and has now given to Clark. However, when he learns that the necklace is formed from a fragment of the meteor that killed her parents, Clark leaves it unobtrusively on Lana's doorstep, even though he knows that he can never be close to her while she wears it.

LEX: You want to tell me what happened last night?
CLARK: It was just a stupid prank.
LEX: You were tied to a stake in the middle of a field. Even the Romans saved that for special occasions.

"We like to alternate between the character scenes and the really scary moments in the show," Al Gough comments. "So we go from a very touching scene in the barn to a kid who's peeling his skin off with steel wool!"

'Metamorphosis' allowed Gough and Millar the chance to explore further some of the themes that they had established in the pilot. "It's an interesting episode in terms of the Lana/Whitney relationship," Millar notes, "and the idea of Lex playing Cupid is a theme that we play with, and really like. In the first season, he's always telling Lana she's dating the wrong guy."

The episode focuses far more strongly on the 'Freak of the Week' — the person affected by kryptonite — than did the pilot. "Kryptonite always weakens Superman," Al Gough explains, "but the thing that we added was that it actually gave regular people superpowers. Otherwise, who is Clark going to fight week to week in a small town?" Gough points out that "the power sort of enhances the characters' sins. They're not

Opposite: Clark carries Whitney from the wreckage of his truck.

monsters, in terms of make-up, but it comes from their personal demons."

Not surprisingly for a show early in its début season and still finding its style, the production came up against a lot of challenges. "That was at a time when the show had to work, so if a scene sucked, we reshot it," Al Gough recalls. For example, Miles Millar wanted either to reshoot or remove the scene where Clark, Pete and Chloe break into the Arkin house: "It looked ridiculous, because Tom had long hair one second, and short hair the next, and then he was back with long hair." Unfortunately someone had cut Tom's hair short, so hair extensions had to be added, which Tom wore until his hair grew back to the right length a few weeks later.

A lot of work was carried out between the end of shooting the pilot and the start of filming on the first episode. "We did a complete makeover at the Kent farm," Rob Maier recalls. "For the pilot, we had only built the kitchen and the dining room, and we then built the whole floor of the house and then some. We had used the farm's barn as a

Smallville Ledger

* * * Volume 63, Number 43 * * *

UNUSUAL WEBS OF SILK FOUND IN SMALLVILLE AREA

Local authorities can offer no plausible explanation for the large strands of silk that have been found in various locations around Smallville in the last few days. The silk, which has been spun into unimaginably huge webs, has been found mostly inside dark, little-used structures such as barns and sheds.

"We sent some of the stuff to M.U. for analysis," said Sheriff Waid, "but we're not quite sure what to make of what they sent back." Frank Lagrepus, adjunct associate professor of entomology at Metropolis University, elaborated: "Preliminary tests indicate that the silk came from some sort of a spider. But an arachnid that could produce this… well, it would have to be magnitudes larger than any species we've ever studied. We may be sending this on to S.T.A.R. Labs for further examination."

By Sandy Maggin

practical location for the pilot, and built a loft and stairs up into that, but for the series we built our own barn. Our designer, Doug Higgins, did a remarkable job — he was very exacting, and a great guy to work for. We researched everything — we have 100-year-old wood in that set, taken from a hand-hewn barn. We have pieces of an old roller coaster in there, and a ton of material from the old Versatile Shipyards in North Vancouver which were built at the turn of the last century."

The producers were delighted with the performance of Chad E. Donella as 'Bug Boy'. "When the villains are good, it helps elevate the rest of the show," Gough points out. "He has an intensity which is very scary and very real." The scene between Clark and Lana in the barn is equally intense. "We call these our 'soul mate' moments," Miles Millar says. "We enjoy writing them, and they're fun."

CLARK: As soon as I woke up, I crashed. I mean, Dad, what's happening to me?

JONATHAN: I honestly don't know. As soon as you start breaking the law of gravity, we're definitely in uncharted territory.

John Schneider liked the teamwork forced on Clark and Whitney at the end of the episode. "They had to get together to save the day, which was great," he says. "You know they didn't want to, but they had to, because they were better people. They rose above their circumstance, joined together and took care of the problem." ■

SMALLVILLE MUSIC

'Save Me' by Remy Zero
'Last Resort' by Papa Roach
'Island In the Sun' by Weezer
'I Do' by Better Than Ezra
'Underdog (Save Me)'
   by Turin Brakes
'Love You Madly' by Cake
'Damaged' by Aeon Spoke
'Wherever You Will Go'
   by The Calling
'Everything' by Lifehouse

HOTHEAD

WRITTEN BY: Greg Walker
DIRECTED BY: Greg Beeman

GUEST STARS: Jason Connery (Dominic Santori), Sarah-Jane Redmond (Nell Potter), John Glover (Lionel Luthor), Dan Lauria (Coach Walt Arnold), Hiro Kanagawa (Principal Kwan), David Paetkau (Trevor Chapel)

DID YOU KNOW?

In John Byrne's 1986 retelling of Superman's origins in the comic book mini-series *Superman: The Man of Steel*, Clark is a local football hero in Smallville, and Jonathan tells him about his alien origins because he's worried that someone will get hurt.

Smallville High football coach Walt is determined to achieve 200 victories, and will do anything to win, including helping his team cheat at exams. New Principal Kwan threatens to disqualify the team members who cheated, prompting the coach to use his meteor-induced power to create fire against him. Clark has finally persuaded his mother to allow him to try out for the team, but Jonathan is worried that Clark will use his powers in the heat of the moment — as he does, to a small extent, in a practice game. Chloe witnesses the coach using his powers to make water sprinklers throw fire across the football field, and the coach tries to kill her by burning down the *Torch* office. After rescuing both Kwan and Chloe, Clark goes to battle the coach, but Walt locks Clark in the sauna with the meteor rocks from which he has gotten his powers. Jonathan releases Clark, and the coach is burned by his own fire.

Meanwhile, Lana quits cheerleading and tries her hand at waitressing, without much success. Lex is ordered by his father to cut twenty percent of his workforce, but finds a way to cut the budget instead.

JONATHAN: I do not want anyone coming on this farm and taking our son away from us.

MARTHA: Well, if we don't start trusting him, nobody's going to have to take him away. He's going to leave all by himself.

"I have about fifty pounds of hairspray in my hair," Allison Mack explains, "so my head is incredibly flammable." Allison's hairstyle became very relevant to this episode, when she volunteered to take part in a stunt where Chloe is set on fire as the *Torch* office is set ablaze. "All our cast is game," stuntman Christopher Sayour points out. "When Chloe got fried, it was Allison inside that burning jacket."

"The fire in the *Torch* [office] was supposed to explode around me," Allison recalls, "but the first time the fire was soft. The second time, I was *completely* surrounded by fire. I had the flaming coat over my head, and I had to throw it off, but it caught around my arm. In the shot you can see me shaking my arm like mad to get it off! That was the first time I was ever rescued by Clark Kent!"

'Hothead' is perhaps most notable for the introduction to the series of director Greg Beeman, who very quickly became a highly valued member of the production crew,

Opposite: Lionel Luthor, fresh from his fencing match with Lex.

Smallville Ledger

* * * Volume 63, Number 44 * * *

LUTHOR SURPRISES FERTILIZER INDUSTRY WITH PLANNED WORKFORCE INCREASE

… plant president Lex Luthor recently commented… "The last thing I want to do is alienate the honest, hardworking people of Smallville, my valued neighbors. On the contrary, I'm here to say that I plan to lift them up, and with them the local economy, to heights not seen since Smallville was the envy of all the heartland."

Rhetoric aside, this reporter must admit a certain admiration for Luthor's nerve at offering to hire more locals rather than put them out. Are we seeing a new business paradigm at work in our humble town? Can Smallville's plant workers expect, dare I say it, a "kinder, gentler" management style from the heir to Lionel Luthor's legacy? Only time will tell. But as they clock in and out each day, surely those employees must be starting to get the sense that Lex Luthor is clearly not cut from the same cloth as his father.

By John K. McGuiness

eventually becoming executive producer later in the season. "I loved his dedication to Superman and to *Smallville*," Joe Davola recalls. "He was an important part of helping us straighten out production up in Vancouver."

"Al and I had worked with Greg on *The Strip* and *Martial Law*," Miles Millar recalls, "and we always thought he would be great for *Smallville*. He came up and did a fantastic job, and I think really helped define the look of the show. He had all the colors we'd always wanted to get."

"In the entirety of *Smallville*, 'Hothead' is not one of the best episodes ever," Greg Beeman admits, "but it's one of the first episodes that got finished relatively on schedule. At least from a visual standpoint, if not a story standpoint, everyone said that this was what they wanted the show to look like on an ongoing basis."

"We still hadn't found our groove yet," Miles Millar notes, "so structurally it's different from the rest of the series. It's three very separate stories, and the Lex, Clark and Lana stories intersect at the coffee shop very randomly."

"The football sequence at the beginning of the episode was one of my favorite days of shooting," Eric Johnson says. "They had the rain towers out to create the rain, and we were shooting at Swan Guard Stadium with some real football players. I just had a blast. I played football in high school and I wasn't very good, but when they cut it together — I look awesome."

John Glover's willingness to try new ideas impressed stunt coordinator Lauro

DID YOU KNOW?

Greg Beeman is a huge comic book fan — he has a collection of over 3,000 comic books in sealed bags that he's kept since he was a boy.

Chartrand when they planned the swordfight between Lex and Lionel. "I wanted to spice it up a little bit and have him jump and roll over the pool table and come around," Chartrand recalls. "I hadn't seen John do anything and he'd never seemed too gung-ho, but once we got into it, he said he could do it. We taught him how to roll smoothly and carried on with the sword fight. He and Michael did a great job."

CHLOE: Clark Kent is a football player and Lana Lang is a waitress.
PETE: What's the matter with that?
CHLOE: Nothing. I just want to click my heels and get back to reality.

As ever, there were certain changes to the script during the writing process. "I was told originally in 'Hothead' that I was going to be the kid that the coach goes after, and he was going to burn my arm," Eric Johnson continues, "but then they realized that they were beating Whitney up every episode!"

"On my second day, we did the scene where Clark saves Principal Kwan from the exploding car," Greg Beeman says. "He rips the door off the car and saves Kwan, and we were doing a bluescreen shot with the car exploding. That was the specific moment when I realized that I loved this show and this was where I belonged! The show was in organizational chaos, but I had this strong gut feeling that I knew what Miles and Al wanted, and I had an instinctive sense that I knew how to get it there, both artistically and organizationally…" ■

SMALLVILLE MUSIC

'Renegade Fighter' by Zed
'Clint Eastwood' by Gorillaz
'Motivation' by Sum 41
'Bad Day' by Fuel
'Never Let You Go'
   by Third Eye Blind
'You' by Binocular

Left: Lex and Lionel cross
swords verbally.

X-RAY

WRITTEN BY: Mark Verheiden
DIRECTED BY: James Frawley

GUEST STARS: Lizzy Caplan (Tina Greer), Tom O'Brien (Roger Nixon), Mark McConchie (Mr Ellis), Sarah-Jane Redmond (Nell Potter), Beverley Breuer (Rose Greer)

Clark tries to foil a robbery at the local bank, apparently carried out by Lex, during which he discovers a new power, X-ray vision, which reveals that 'Lex' has an unusual skeleton. 'Lex' escapes and morphs into Tina Greer, a teenager whose brittle bones were affected by the meteor shower. Tina accidentally causes her mother's death, and then tries to persuade Lana that they should move in together, as Tina feels they are like sisters. As Clark tries to train his eyes to use his X-ray vision, Martha visits Tina's mother's shop, where she spots money from the bank robbery. Tina then impersonates Clark in an attempt to kill her. Clark spots the rest of the money in her locker, but Tina gets away from the police, then tries to kill Lana so she can assume her friend's perfect life. Clark battles Tina and rescues Lana.

Lana finds her mother's old diary, and learns that her mother didn't have the perfect life that Lana thought she had. Investigative reporter Roger Nixon tries to blackmail Lex, but the young tycoon turns the tables and forces Nixon to work for him, investigating Lex's amazing survival of the car crash.

LANA: Have you ever tried to find your parents? Your biological parents, I mean.

CLARK: Not really. I figure they're a million years away from my life now.

"X-ray vision had always been 'see-through' vision in all the previous incarnations of the franchise," Miles Millar points out. "It's been super-vision: the wall melted away, and then you saw through to the other space. It wasn't X-ray vision. We wanted to do real X-ray vision, and see the skeletons and the bones."

With every new power that appears on the series, executive producers Al Gough and Miles Millar work very closely with the effects house to ensure that their vision is brought to the screen. "We go down to the effects house for days looking at what they do," Millar explains. "We spent a long time working on the visual effects of the X-rays, and they work really well."

Whenever they talk about the series as a whole, Gough and Millar point to this episode as the one where the structure of the show started to come together. "We really struggled with this episode for a long time, and finally got it right," Millar says. "It's the first episode which we really think is a good paradigm for the show. All the stories link nicely. It has the nice B-story for Lana with her mother and the tape of her speech at the prom which began to unravel Lana's own secrets. And Tina Greer was one of our favorite bad guys — we brought her back later because we thought she was a fun

Opposite: Tina Greer disguises herself as Whitney to get close to Lana.

MUSIC

'Movies' by Alien Ant Farm
'Ooh La La' by The Wiseguys
'Breathe You In' by
  Stabbing Westward
'Analyze' by The Cranberries
'Unbroken' by Todd Thibaud
'Up All Night' by Unwritten Law
'Wall In Your Heart' by Shelby Lynne

character, and Lizzie Caplan did a really good job."

"What we've discovered is that it's not the best way to do *Smallville* to have wildly divergent B-stories, where people are just off on their own tangents," writer Mark Verheiden says. "It helps make the stories feel richer and more thematic if most of the characters at least have some effect on each other. 'X-Ray' was the first time where we dovetailed the B-stories into the main story, so that whatever action was happening in the A-story was affecting everyone, not just Clark or Lana."

The episode saw Christopher Sayour's first work on the show as Tom Welling's stunt double. "It was a pretty wild stunt," Sayour recalls. "I had to come through the loft double doors. Tina pushes Clark, he smashes through the doors and falls about twelve feet through the windshield of a truck. It was very specific how they wanted it, and a very difficult day, but the producers loved it, and Tom loved it!"

Stunt coordinator Lauro Chartrand recalls that another stuntman didn't have as much luck when he was doubling for Clark during the bank raid. "I'll be damned if they

SMALLVILLE TORCH

Volume 50, Number 45

TORCH TORMENTED

So the *Torch* was torched, but as promised, I'm back. As a wave of flames nipped at my heels, I started thinking... what is it with Smallville?

Do a quick math problem with me. October 16, 1989 — D.O.S. (Day of Shower). Meteors fall from the sky, decimating the idyllic hamlet of Smallville. Post-D.O.S. — weird stuff starts to happen. Don't believe me? Let's add up a few of the freaky events of the past month.

Take one Jeremy Creek in a coma since D.O.S. — dorky kid, aged exactly no days, shows up at Homecoming unconscious at the wheel of a crashed truck. Add to Jeremy one Greg Arkin — mom found dead, entombed in a 'spider' web. But then subtract Greg Arkin, because he hasn't been seen since. Add in one legendary football coach going for win 200, but don't get too attached, because you have to subtract him, too. Unfortunately, coach mysteriously disappeared in a fire after his players named him in a schoolwide cheating scandal. Multiply it all by Tina Greer — found impersonating a football star and trying to kill Lana Lang. Conveniently, we've got to subtract her too because she was shipped off to an asylum to work on her identity crisis. What's the sum of all that craziness? One seriously screwed-up small town.

By Chloe Sullivan

didn't have a malfunction on the air ram," he says, referring to the compressed air device which accelerates the stuntman away from it with a great deal of force. "The stunt guy has to be committed when you go off these things, and he jumped in time with the air ram, and it didn't go off at all. He came way short of his mark — he didn't make it to the window, thank goodness — and hit his head on the wall," he says. "He was expecting to be thrown back fourteen feet through a glass window and onto some pads. You should have seen the look on his face when his ass hit the concrete! He just got up and started swearing. He was so determined and so prepared — and it didn't happen. To his credit, he got up, we got the air ram figured out, we did it, and it was great."

CLARK: Mom, if you could see anything, what would you do?
MARTHA: Learn to close my eyes.

The final battle between Clark and Tina Greer in the graveyard was reshot to make it more dramatically effective. "The first time we did it, it was all way too cartoony," Miles Millar recalls. "We had people flipping over gravestones, and it was very *Buffy*-esque." "The ending wasn't very cinematic," Greg Beeman explains, "and I said that I had an idea for the fight. I wanted to make it like the two Terminators fighting each other, bashing in the headstones — so we went back and reshot the ending like that." ∎

DID YOU KNOW?

Many of the exterior scenes on Smallville's main street are filmed in the town of Cloverdale, a few miles southeast of Vancouver. The town now has its own Smallville Antiques store, next door to the Clover cinema, which doubles as the Talon.

COOL

| WRITTEN BY: Michael Green | GUEST STARS: Michael Coristine (Sean Kelvin), |
| DIRECTED BY: James A. Contner | Tania Saulnier (Jenna) |

An accident during a winter party sends womanizing student Sean Kelvin to the bottom of frozen, meteor-infested Crater Lake, and when he emerges, he can only get warm by absorbing heat from objects and people around him. He seduces Jenna, a fellow student, then steals her body heat from her, literally freezing her to death. His next target is Chloe. Lex tries to aid the Kents and invites them to the mansion to offer them financial assistance with the farm. With Whitney otherwise engaged, Lana agrees to go to a Radiohead concert with Clark, just as friends, and courtesy of Lex, but Clark abandons her when he realizes that Chloe is in trouble. He saves Chloe, then follows Sean's trail to the mansion, where he prevents Sean from killing his parents and Lex before sending Sean to the bottom of Crater Lake once more. Jonathan decides to take out a bank loan rather than go into partnership with Lex.

LEX: This is the perfect time for you to ask her out.
CLARK: She's got a boyfriend, Lex.
LEX: A high school boyfriend isn't a husband. He's an obstacle.

"'Cool' was one of the first episodes where the notion that kryptonite enhances the sin of the afflicted came into serious play," writer Mark Verheiden recalls. "The 'cool' kid literally became cool, needing human body heat to stay alive. While none of the early episodes were easy to figure out — the joy of working out first season kinks — I don't recall that the basic concept of 'Cool' changed much once we got started."

Miles Millar believes this is another of the early episodes in which certain themes started to be explored, and in which certain other problems became clearer. "I like the idea behind Chloe's story," he comments. "'Cool' started this run of stories in which Chloe always falls in love with the wrong guy. That was a fun way to broaden the horizons. The episode was entertaining, and a different way to tell the Freak of the Week story, but the end is a bit unsatisfying. You don't know where the kid is. Did Clark kill him? We had a struggle initially in the show. We didn't want to see Clark kill anybody, but he needed to be able to defeat the bad guys. It's something that we addressed later, but 'Cool' is a case in point. At the end of the show, where do the bad guys go? In that episode, Clark tosses him into the water, and it freezes — so what does that mean?"

In order to make the best possible show, the producers would require reshoots of scenes that might not work as well as they could. "We were going overbudget," Joe Davola recalls, "and the studio was getting a little flipped about that. We were pushing the crew beyond our limits. We were freezing lakes when it wasn't freezing cold. But there was such a desire from everyone to get it right that we kept on doing it and moving

Opposite: Clark and Jonathan consider the future.

SMALLVILLE TORCH

Volume 50, Number 46

BIZARRE CHAIN OF EVENTS CULMINATES AT LUTHOR ESTATE

... Mark 'Wink' Waid, the sheriff of Smallville, was visibly shaken, refusing to give many details upon emerging from Lex Luthor's massive front gate. Security was unusually high both there and at the Kelvin home, with no photographers or reporters allowed in and no eyewitnesses available. Strangely, rescue workers arrived at the Luthor home with large pickaxes, but no bodies had been brought out at press time.

Seemingly on the verge of nausea, Waid said, "I wish I could give you folks something you could print... In my eight years as this town's sheriff, I've never seen anything like what I just witnessed here and at Sean's place. Trust me, you don't want photos." With that, the well-liked sheriff slumped into the arms of his deputies and was led to a waiting cruiser.

By Christopher James Beppo

things on. Everyone was looking for a hit, so in the beginning, the vaults were open for us to overspend and get what we needed."

As always, stunt coordinator Lauro Chartrand tried to ensure that the fight sequence between Clark and the villain featured as much of the real actors as possible. "We always tried to use Tom for everything," he explains. "If it was a bigger stunt, and he was being thrown, I'd always give the producers a piece of Tom leading into it. You'd see him being thrown, and then we'd chuck him off some boxes, which would give them a good energetic shot of his face, and then we'd put stuntman Christopher Sayour on a ratchet or an air ramp, and then they could cut to the wider shot of Christopher flying through the air. And in any of the fighting that led up to him being thrown, Tom was always in there."

LEX: Your son brought me back from the dead, Mr. Kent. When he reached in and pulled me out, he gave me a new life. Your father put his family's future over his own pride. Are you willing to do that?

Chartrand was always delighted that the guest stars enjoyed the physicality of their roles, which particularly helped, given the speed of shooting on *Smallville*. "At any one time in those early days, I'd be cleaning up a previous episode — adding on to a stunt or redoing a big stunt — I'd be doing stunts on the current episode, and I'd have to prep the next one coming up," he remembers. "Casting would go right down to the wire, so we'd start prepping the episode without knowing who was going to play the part. I'd ask

SMALLVILLE MUSIC

'Rescue' by Eve 6
'Let Your Shoulder Fall' by Matthew Jay
'We're At the Top of the World' by the Juliana Theory
'On Your Side' by Pete Yorn
'Standing Still' by Jewel
'This Way' by Jewel

Opposite: Chloe falls for the wrong guy.

for a picture and size as soon as possible so I could get a good double. But most of the guest stars were young athletic kids who could do the stunts for the most part. They were all pretty excited. I never ran into one who didn't want to do it. They would do as much as I would allow them to do." ∎

HOURGLASS

WRITTEN BY: Doris Egan
DIRECTED BY: Chris Long

GUEST STARS: George Murdock (Old Harry), Eric Christian Olsen (Young Harry), Jackie Burroughs (Cassandra Carver), Mitchell Kosterman (Sheriff Ethan)

Clark, Pete and Lana are helping out at a local retirement center, where the boys meet Cassandra Carver, who, ever since the meteor shower, has been able to tell people's futures by touching them. Lana is looking after elderly Harry Bollston, who is rejuvenated when he falls into a pond containing meteor rocks. Bollston is really Harry Volk, a convicted murderer, who decides to use his newfound youth to gain revenge on the descendants of those responsible for his conviction. Cassandra touches Clark and warns him that someone close to him will die. A second vision shows Clark standing alone in a graveyard containing the tombs of his friends and family, while a third sees him helping people. Clark saves Harry's target in the nick of time, and hands the young man over to the police, but everyone is surprised when the next day old Harry is in his hospital bed. Harry returns to the pond, rejuvenates himself again, and goes after Hiram Kent's descendant, Jonathan. Clark and Jonathan arrive just in time to rescue Martha, who has lured Harry into the silo, in which he drowns in corn. Lex, intrigued by Clark's story about Cassandra, finally agrees to let her touch him. Her vision is of death and destruction at Lex's hands, which triggers her death — she herself was the person that she told Clark was fated to die.

LANA: Do you know anyone else who's lost an entire old person in a wheelchair?

CHLOE: No... that's pretty impressive, even by Smallville standards.

'Hourglass' is nominated by many of the cast as their favorite episode from the early part of the series. It's a particular favorite with the older generation, and as John Schneider points out, "We know what it was like to be young, but the younger people don't know what it's like to be older. Our perspective is entirely different. That was an excellent show — that young man did a great job."

Guest star Eric Christian Olsen was delighted with the opportunity to appear in *Smallville*, playing "the nemesis of Superman who tries to kill his father and his mother! There's a shot in the episode of old Harry going into the water as a seventy-year-old man, and morphing into a seventeen-year-old boy — me. They said, 'We want that shot.' It was after the main filming had finished, so they flew me back to Vancouver, for two days, for one shot. I went in there for two days, I put my head in the water, I smiled, and I pulled my head out, and that was it. They're perfectionists — that's why the show is so successful."

Annette O'Toole clearly remembers filming the climactic fight between her and

Opposite: Clark must face a vision of his future.

Olsen in the corn silo, which was shot at the P.N.E. (Pacific National Exhibition), a large area of Vancouver that contains a massive funfair. "We were in this funny little mock-silo," she says, "and they were pouring this stuff in on us. It was freezing, and I remember being really rigid and not being able to breathe, because I couldn't breathe the corn in through the tube."

'Hourglass' was one of the original five pitches that Gough and Millar came up with for the network, back when they needed to show sample stories they'd use if *Smallville* was picked up as a series. "It took us a long time to break this story," Miles Millar recalls, using the industry term for coming up with a plotline that fits the TV episode format. "It has two stories going on. It's not a true crime story, but there are elements of a true crime story in there. You've got the old man falling into the Fountain of Youth, and then he becomes a serial killer. At the same time you have Cassandra at the old peoples' home." "I think we hit our groove on 'Hourglass'," Joe Davola adds. "We didn't bite off more than we could chew, and creatively it wasn't Freak of the Week."

Greg Beeman describes 'Hourglass' as "the first of the really mythological episodes since the pilot." Mark Verheiden recalls sitting around a monitor watching the stunning visual effects sequence at the end of the episode. "I think it was the first time we realized

---

Clark's vision

Clark's eyes widen as a blinding blue-white FLASH propels him into a visceral

VISION OF THE FUTURE!
It's like a nightmare, liquid and blurred at the edges. Sheets of rain HAMMER down. Suddenly, a ribbon of lightning razors the night revealing AN OLD MARBLE HEADSTONE. Although sheeted with water and choked with vines, the engraving chiseled into its face is hauntingly visible.

'IN MEMORY OF JONATHAN KENT, BELOVED HUSBAND AND FATHER'
Another flash illuminates Clark standing in front of the headstone. Riverlets of water run down his cheeks as his fingers gently trace the worn letters. As he stands back another lightning flash illuminates a second headstone, this one is dedicated to —

'MARTHA KENT, BELOVED WIFE AND MOTHER'
He spins away, but there's no escape as a violent succession of flashes illuminate headstones belonging to — 'CHLOE SULLIVAN'... 'PETER ROSS'... and 'LANA LANG'. Clark lifts his head to the heavens, opens his mouth in a primeval scream. As the CAMERA SPIRALS UP through the rain, we see he's standing in the middle of a graveyard that stretches into eternity.

just how really great the show could be. It wasn't just going to be cool or interesting — it was going to be really great."

LEX: Then the question you've got to ask yourself is... do you really want to know the future?

CLARK: Don't you wish you knew how it was all going to turn out?

LEX: Life's a journey, Clark. I don't want to go through it following a road map.

Greg Beeman worked with director Chris Long on the two big effects sequences, described in the script as 'visceral visions of the future'. "Our second unit and reshoots were getting so far behind that our directors weren't ever able to stay to finish their episodes," Beeman recalls, "so I participated with Chris quite a bit on those scenes. We did color storyboards for the blood rain, described in the script as: 'As [Lex] touches one of the flowers it withers and dies, sending a cancerous wave of death rippling out across the field, laying waste to everything in its path. Suddenly, A BLOOD RED DROP falls from the deep blue sky, stains his suit. Then another falls, and another and another, until the sky is raining red. As he opens his mouth to scream, there's a flash of white.'"

The scenes of Lex in the White House were filmed on the set of the hit political series *The West Wing*, in Los Angeles. "We called producer John Wells, and he kindly gave us access to the set," Millar recalls. "It was always scripted — we'd always wanted to do that scene, and at the back of our heads, we thought that maybe we could get access to the *West Wing* set. We put it in, hoping John Wells would let us do it, and he did. That was very nice of him." ▪

SMALLVILLE MUSIC

'5/4' by Gorillaz
'Time Served' by Dispatch
Piano Sonata No.3 in B minor, op. 59, and *Piano Sonata No.1* in C minor, op. 4, by Chopin, performed by Idil Beret

CRAVING

WRITTEN BY: Michael Green
DIRECTED BY: Phil Sgriccia

GUEST STARS: Amy Adams (Jodi Melville), Sarah-Jane Redmond (Nell Potter), Joe Morton (Dr. Steven Hamilton), Malcolm Stewart (Jodi's Father)

Overweight teenager Jodi Melville has tried every diet to lose weight, and is amazed when a smoothie of meteor-infected vegetables seems to work. However, along with the weight loss comes an incredible hunger, and soon mountains of junk food are not sufficient. Knocking down a deer in her car, she drains its body fat, but even that doesn't stem the cravings, as her weight continues to plummet. Now that she is thin and attractive to the other students, she has little difficulty persuading one to make out with her, and she steals his body fat, leaving him in a coma. Pete has invited Jodi to accompany him to Lana's birthday party at the Luthor mansion, at which Clark has offered to be Lana's chaperone since Whitney has a tryout for the Metropolis Sharks. As Pete arrives to take her to the party, Jodi's hunger pangs hit her again, and she tries to persuade Pete to leave her alone. He refuses, and she is about to attack him when Clark arrives. They battle in the greenhouse, which explodes, knocking Jodi out. Clark has missed Lana's party, but still is able to give her his birthday gift — their own drive-in movie.

Meanwhile, Lex discovers that his white blood cell count is high, which may be linked to his exposure to the meteor shower. He hires disgraced scientist Dr. Steven Hamilton to investigate the meteor rocks.

CLARK: Having a birthday party at Lex's mansion seems pretty cool to me.
LANA: It stopped being my party a long time ago. If it was up to me, it would be pizza and loud music with my friends.

"'Craving' is one of my favorite early episodes, because it was the first one that I really had a lot of stuff to do in," Sam Jones III maintains. "The Freak of the Week was basically after me, so that was very exciting for me to do."

"I was very happy with the casting of Jodi," Miles Millar notes. "I was never really happy with the script, and if we hadn't cast her, we would have been in deep trouble. But it's interesting, because this was one of our most popular episodes with teens. It did really well in the ratings, and got a great response from teens."

Greg Beeman recalls that this was an episode where the series was still finding its feet. "Amy Adams was great," he says. "It had some cool stuff in it, but I think we were finding our way. Who were our villains? What was appropriate? What wasn't appropriate? I know some people like it, and it deals with some teenage girl issues about food, but I thought it was a little creepy."

The sequence where Jodi hits the deer was the most problematic. Stunt coordinator

Opposite: Birthday girl Lana Lang.

CRAVING

Lauro Chartrand recalls that "one of my best friends, Melissa Stubbs, doubled the girl, when she does a three-sixty in her jeep. I told her it was a night shoot. It was cold and rainy, and they were using rain towers as well. I told her she'd be in and out quickly. The director had other things in mind. He wanted the girl to come out and eat this deer on the road, but he didn't want to put Amy Adams through it. They were shooting it mostly wide, so they got Mel to get out and crawl on her hands and knees up to this stuffed deer and start chewing on it, getting mouthfuls of hair. She got soaked each time!"

CLARK: What do you think it is, Chloe — some fat-sucking vampire in town?

CHLOE: This is Smallville, Clark — land of the weird, home of the strange.

It was one of those episodes where the production schedule caught up with the airing schedule, and there wasn't time to rectify anything that the producers would have preferred to improve upon. "We had the effect of the deer come in on the day of transmission," Miles Millar recalls, "and we couldn't cut around it."

When a television episode is put together, about a week before it is transmitted, the picture is 'locked', which means, among other things, that the composer can write his

Below: Lex in front of the 'Wall of Weird'.

music to the exact time of each scene. Any changes made after that time can only replace a shot with something absolutely identical in terms of length — there isn't an opportunity to re-edit a sequence so that if something is wrong, it can be removed. Unfortunately, that's what happened here. "The deer is a little claymation hairless creature, which turns toward the car," Millar remembers. "It was just too late to change it. I think it's the worst effect we've ever done. If we'd known what the effect was going to be like, we would have found a way to cut around it, but there was no time."

Mark Snow's incidental music added immeasurably to the episode, and was one element on which the producers knew they could always rely. "Miles and I had always loved Mark's work from *The X-Files*," Al Gough comments, "and we very much wanted him to do this show when we got it. He agreed to do it, and I think he liked it and could see that he could do something different on this show than what he'd been doing on *Millennium*. He just does a fantastic job. We give him the shows to score, Mark goes off to his little workshop in Santa Monica and basically delivers fantastic scores week after week, so we don't see him that often! We couldn't be happier to have him." ∎

SMALLVILLE MUSIC

'Slide' by Dido
'Innocent' by Fuel
'Invisible' by Third Eye Blind
'The Fool' by Call and Response
'Hero' by Enrique Iglesias

SMALLVILLE TORCH

Volume 50, Number 47

SMALLVILLE: AMERICA'S STRANGEST TOWN

Over the last couple of weeks, I've laid the theories out for you. I put the question to the people to help me figure out why Smallville has quickly become America's strangest town. From 1989 on, things have gotten pretty whack funky around here, and some of you out there seem to feel the same way as I do. The following are some of the theories you've sent in to me. I've withheld my commentary on each so you can come to your own conclusions...

Theory #2
Sender Name: Maude
Title: Conspiracy Theory
I think that there's one factor in the 'What's wrong with Smallville?' equation that you can't dismiss: cheerleaders. Now, I know that we've had cheerleaders since long before both the meteor shower and the opening of the Luthor plant, but you have to put two and two together.

This is a long-term plan that the cheerleaders have set into motion. They began early this century, cheering their devious battle cry, "Fight, fight, fight!" This incessant call to violence has long weighed on the subconscious of our citizens.

Now, after years of violent and incendiary cheerleader propaganda and subliminal programming, the citizens are ripe for the cheerleaders' evil bidding. Their most loyal devotees? The football team. Notice anything strange about our beloved coach? Tina Greer tried to infiltrate their ranks, and where did it land her? Any coincidence that Lana Lang seems to be at the center of these mysterious events? I think not.

By Chloe Sullivan

JITTERS

WRITTEN BY: Cherie Bennett & Jeff Gottesfeld

DIRECTED BY: Michael Watkins

GUEST STARS: John Glover (Lionel Luthor), Robert Wisden (Gabe Sullivan), Tony Todd (Earl Jenkins), Mitchell Kosterman (Sheriff Ethan)

DID YOU KNOW?

Tony Todd is a very familiar face to science fiction and horror audiences, headlining the *Candyman* series of movies, and appearing in everything from *Star Trek* to *Xena: Warrior Princess*.

Janitor Earl Jenkins is desperate to discover the cause of the violent shaking that kills anyone who comes too close to him, before it kills him. He turns for help to the Kents, but only Clark is at home, hosting a party that has gotten out of control while his parents celebrate their wedding anniversary in Metropolis. On their return, Earl tells Jonathan that he believes he was infected while cleaning Level 3 at the LutherCorp Fertilizer Plant. However, he has been told that Level 3 doesn't exist. Chloe's father is supervisor at the plant and has invited her class to visit, and when they do, they are taken hostage by Earl, who demands the truth. Lionel Luthor flies in, furious that Lex has allowed this to happen. Lex goes into the plant to assure Earl that Level 3 doesn't exist, and exchanges himself for the hostages. Clark secretly stays behind and finds the elevator that Earl was sure existed. Earl, Lex and Clark go down to Level 3, now an abandoned hangar, no longer filled with the meteor rock-fed plants that Earl saw. Although Earl's meteor-created condition saps Clark's strength, he is able to save the others when a gantry is shaken beyond its limits by Earl's jitters. Furious that his father lied to him about Level 3, Lex publicly announces that LutherCorp will fund Earl's medical treatment.

CLARK: I heard there was a third level to the plant. Is that true?
GABE SULLIVAN: Yeah, yeah. That's where we do the alien autopsies.

"'Jitters' was a massive undertaking," Miles Millar comments, "which turned out well, but it was very traumatic to shoot."

The episode had originally been intended as the second episode to air after the pilot, but ended up as the eighth broadcast episode after it became clear that a considerable amount of reshoots were necessary to make it work. "It was actually shot second but abandoned," Greg Beeman recalls. "When we watched it in the cut, we realized that it didn't make sense, so we decided to reconceive it, and fill in the missing gaps. The problem was that the jitters guy himself was supposed to be a sympathetic character, but he was completely unlikable. He had virtually no scenes, and then he was a raving maniac. How were you meant to empathize with this guy? So we added in the scene at the beginning where he's looking down at the little baby. That was a new scene, which was very important. I went back and did a lot of work with Tony Todd, who was great about playing Earl as more empathetic."

The final version of the episode contains work from numerous different directors. "I wanted to match the work of the original director," Greg Beeman notes. "It was

Opposite: Lana turns to Whitney for support during the siege.

SMALLVILLE MUSIC

'Pacific Coast Party'
by Smashmouth
'Tie Me Up' by Handsome Devil
'Bad Idea' by Bad Ronald
'The People That We Love' by Bush
'My Bridges Burn' by The Cult

important to match the tone and the look so that it feels like there is a unity. Phil Sgriccia directed the final battle sequence. Michael Watkins directed the really beautiful stuff at the very end, where he had Lex observing the Kent family. There was a sense of isolation, and you really got the sense of where Lex was going with his life. His father had betrayed him, and in contrast here were the Kents."

"Tony Todd was up here in Vancouver for about a month," Annette O'Toole recalls, and Sam Jones III remembers being surprised when he ran into him in one of Vancouver's main shopping streets. Greg Beeman describes filming 'Jitters' as "like putting together a puzzle", and for that to work, Tony Todd had to be available as various portions of the episode were shot. "The final sequence on the gantry was originally shot on one of those fateful evenings when we were running out of time, and the plug got pulled before they dropped the gantry to the floor," construction coordinator Rob Maier recalls. "We finished it off at an old boiler-making factory and eventually crashed the gantry to the ground. The two pieces meld together, and with all the visual effects, it all turned out well."

'Jitters' was the first episode Mitchell Kosterman, playing the then-unnamed sheriff, worked on. "I was involved in all three parts of filming on that," Kosterman says. "I remember that they gave me this silly sheriff's hat which I didn't like — the wardrobe department always has their own idea of how you should look. But Michael Watkins took it off my head, threw it over the door of the hospital where we were shooting and said, 'No hats!'"

Below: Clark finds the plans of the LuthorCorp plant.

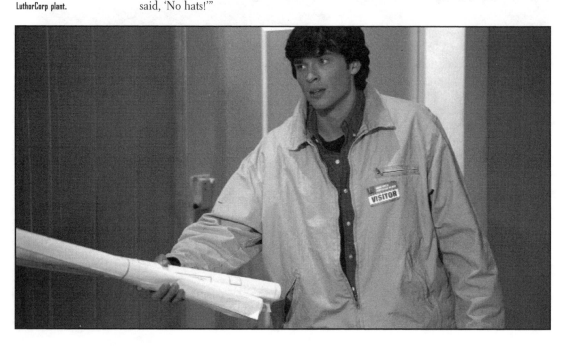

Smallville ✦ Ledger

★ ★ ★ Volume 63, Number 49 ★ ★ ★

WE DON'T NEED ANOTHER HERO?

Reprinted from the weekly *Inquisitor* column 'What No One Else Is Telling You'.

... let's revisit a real rising star, Smallville businessman Lex Luthor. I was simply stunned when Stumpy, the *Inquisitor*'s beloved forty-two-year-old mailboy, dropped off a huge stack of poison-pen letters from *Ledger* readers responding to my harmless piece from a few issues ago. I had no idea Lex had already stirred up such controversy during his short tenure at the fertilizer plant, but I guess the smaller the town, the deeper the emotions.

Most of what I received is unprintable (and some of it's just plain illegible), but the gist was along the lines of, "We don't need a savior in Smallville." Well, let me tell you something, after the recent debacle out at the fertilizer plant, I say you do need a hero, Smallville, and you've got one, like it or not...

... A little footnote for those of you who persist in searching and scrutinizing, desperately trying to pin something on Lex: A cursory glance at the hostage-taker's employment record will tell you that if this so-called "Level 3" ever really existed, it was created long before Lex took over the plant. The business that Lex Luthor is guiding to success is squeaky clean and free of the corruption and sleaze that marks the elder Luthor's reign. Yes, the apple does fall far from the tree — about as far as the squat Smallville Fertilizer Plant No.#3 is from the gleaming glass-and-steel monstrosity in Metropolis known as LuthorCorp Tower.

By *Inquisitor* columnist Roger Nixon

Scriptwriters Cherie Bennett and Jeff Gottesfeld were surprised to be handed the hostage drama. "We went through the quickest learning curve on writing a hostage drama in history," Gottesfeld recalls. "We spent the entire weekend watching every hostage drama film that had ever been made. It was not a genre with which we were greatly familiar — but now we are!"

LEX: My father doesn't care about you. He doesn't care about anybody in this room. Because if we all die, his P.R. firm will spin it, his insurance company will pay out, and you, Earl, will go down as the bad guy.

"We had been labeled as the Freak of the Week show," Miles Millar says, "and we had put 'Jitters' earlier because it was different. But then when it played where it did, it answered the question of whether we just did those stories. It was an expensive episode to produce, but I think it really pays off." ∎

DID YOU KNOW?

Although most people think of 'Rogue' as the first time that *Smallville* visits Metropolis, 'Jitters' actually has that honor — Jonathan and Martha head there for their wedding anniversary.

ROGUE

WRITTEN BY: Mark Verheiden
DIRECTED BY: David Carson

GUEST STARS: Kelly Brook (Victoria Hardwick), Cameron Dye (Sam Phelan), Hiro Kanagawa (Principal Kwan), Mitchell Kosterman (Sheriff Ethan)

While taking a break from a party at the Metropolis Museum, at which Lex meets his old flame Victoria Hardwick, Clark stops a bus from hitting a homeless man. Although he believes no one saw him, he was in fact spotted by corrupt cop Sam Phelan, who tracks him down to Smallville and blackmails Clark into helping him steal files from the home of the Internal Affairs Division's chief. Clark travels to Metropolis with him, but then dumps the entire safe on Phelan. The cop manages to talk his way out of it, and frames Jonathan for murder. He tells Clark he'll arrange for the murder charge to be dropped if Clark steals the jewel-encrusted breastplate of Alexander the Great from the museum. Lex follows them to Metropolis, and calls security. Clark escapes as Phelan is killed in a gunfight with the police, refusing to tell Lex what hold he had over Clark.

Meanwhile, Principal Kwan fires Chloe from the *Torch*, and Lana reluctantly replaces her — only to be fired in her turn and Chloe reinstated by the principal when Lana's first story discusses his crushing Chloe's freedom of speech.

PHELAN: You have a secret you don't want the world to know about. I'm guessing that's why you didn't stick around for the TV cameras last night. You want to keep things that way, you'll do as I say.

"It was fun to play with a hero who makes teenage mistakes and puts his own family in jeopardy," writer Mark Verheiden notes. "'Rogue' was very difficult for us to figure out, but we all felt that it was a good change-up for us, because it showed that we could do non-Freak of the Week episodes and do more emotional stories."

The episode certainly marks a difference in the series, as everything seems to shift up a gear. "It was one of the first really mature storylines," Kristin Kreuk comments. "It was more adult-based than teenager-based. It's probably because it's the first story set in Metropolis, and when Clark's anger came out, it gave him a lot more depth and layers."

"'Rogue' was our first total true crime story," Miles Millar explains. "It was one of the episodes where everything really came together well. The casting was really good, the story was really good, the director was great, and we had a phenomenal opening sequence with the bus. It was also the first episode that Bob Hargrove, who became our line producer, was in charge of. Things were beginning to click."

For the first time there were extensive scenes in Metropolis. In DC Comics continuity, Metropolis often looks like a much sunnier and brighter place, compared to grim Gotham City. "Our Metropolis is definitely not sunny Smallville," Millar says. "It's

Opposite: Lady Victoria Hardwick.

much more metallic and modern, and it always has an urban edge. The colors are different as well — we use much more silver and black. Where Smallville is saturated with color, Metropolis is monochromatic. It gives a different feel, and it's definitely darker than [director] Richard Donner's version in the 1978 *Superman* movie."

Greg Beeman was delighted to get the services of David Carson as a director. Carson had "awesome credits with visual effects work, but what I did not know was what a great performance director he was," the producer comments. "Previous to that, Tom had always had charisma and always was inherently likeable, but he was really nervous and inexperienced as an actor. But David Carson was the first guy to come in here and work the actors. He got an angry intensity out of Tom that none of us knew he could do. In some ways, 'Rogue' was probably the genesis of what would later become 'Red Clark' — Tom Welling when he plays dark."

The story hits at one of the keynote themes for the series — what happens if someone learns Clark's secret? "It was the first time that someone had really come after Clark," Miles Millar notes. "We'd always dealt with the freaks, but this was much more personal to Clark."

"We spent quite a while breaking the episode," Mark Verheiden recalls, "because it

SMALLVILLE MUSIC

'Breathing' by Lifehouse
'Everything' by Lifehouse
'Step It Up' by Stereo MCs
'I Have Seen' by Zero 7
'Angel' by Massive Attack
'She Lives By the Water' by Club 8
'Numb' by Grant Park
'Take Your Time' by Radford

SMALLVILLE TORCH

Volume 50, Number 50

KWAN CRUSHES FREEDOM OF SPEECH

It's the First Amendment of the Constitution of the United States of America. It's one of the defining freedoms of our great country. It's freedom of speech. And Principal James Kwan just crushed it.

Last Tuesday, SHS's principal James Kwan suspended *Torch* editor-in-chief Chloe Sullivan because she wrote an article entitled "Smallville: Mutant Capital of the World." Kwan's reasoning was that "Miss Sullivan was not reporting on relevant school events and was passing the *Torch* off as her own personal tabloid." Unfortunately for Smallville, Chloe's "speculations" are a lot closer to hard news than they are to "tabloid" journalism.

If our high schools are incubating microcosms meant to prepare us for "real-world America", then our administration is playing the part of a leader slightly to the right of Joseph Stalin and Adolf Hitler. The *Torch* is *our* press. Students don't have to read it if they don't want to. That's also one of our freedoms. If S.H.S.'s administration fails to act as a responsible example of authority in line with the government of the United States of America, what message does that send us as students learning how to be productive citizens?

We here at the *Torch* choose to exercise another right guaranteed to us in Amendment One of the Constitution. We hereby petition our administration to redress the grievance of removing Chloe Sullivan from her post as editor-in-chief of the *Torch*. We want her back. It's our right to demand it. It's your responsibility to do something about it.

By Lana Lang

Above: Clark and Lex look at Alexander the Great's breastplate.

was the first one without a kryptonite villain at the center. It took a lot of thinking about how a guy could get something on Clark — he's Superboy! He can zip around and clobber the guy, or do whatever he wants. To me, the coolest scene in that episode is when you finally see that trace of Clark's anger, when he's mad at himself. It's also fun that he screws up twice. Jonathan gets arrested and framed for murder — all kinds of terrible things happen in that one."

LANA: I'm in way over my head. All I wanted to do is help Chloe out and now I feel like I've completely screwed up everything. I guess that's what you get when you try to be a hero.

CLARK: I know the feeling.

'Rogue' also marked the début of Kelly Brook as Victoria Hardwick. The British actress, best known in her home country for her work on the early morning show *The Big Breakfast*, was just starting out on her career in Hollywood, and the show was an important break for her. ∎

SHIMMER

WRITTEN BY: Michael Green
& Mark Verheiden
DIRECTED BY: D.J. Caruso

GUEST STARS: Kelly Brook (Victoria Hardwick), Azura Skye (Amy Palmer), Kett Turton (Jeff Palmer), John Glover (Lionel Luthor), Sarah-Jane Redmond (Nell Potter), Glynis Davies (Mrs. Palmer), Jesse Hutch (Todd Turner)

DID YOU KNOW?

Azura Skye, who plays Amy Palmer, had already appeared with Michael Rosenbaum in another hit WB series, *Zoe, Duncan, Jack & Jane*, as his character Jack's sister, Jane.

Victoria has moved in with Lex while they apparently plan a coup against their respective fathers. This hasn't pleased Amy Palmer, the daughter of the mansion's housekeeper, who has a crush on Lex. There are various attacks within the mansion: Victoria's room is vandalized, and an invisible figure tries to drown her in the bath. Clark and Lex discover that Amy has been stealing from him, and find a shrine to Lex in her room. Rather than press charges, Lex suggests that the Palmers leave, but it's not the end of the problems. Amy's brother Jeff is the real culprit — covering himself in meteor-infected sap which has turned him invisible, he attacks a fellow student who made fun of Amy, and he goes after Lex for not returning his sister's love. Clark battles and eventually defeats Jeff.

Both Clark and Lionel are concerned about Lex's affair with Victoria — Clark found her snooping in Lex's computer, while Lionel warns Lex against battling him. Clark and Lana become closer during the school blood drive, but when Clark discovers that Whitney has not been confiding in Lana because he is worried about his father's illness, he tells her that Whitney needs her.

> **JONATHAN: Clark, uh… I can't even believe I'm actually going to say this, but I guess you can't always be honest with people. It's one of the prices you pay for your abilities.**

"'Shimmer' is an interesting episode, because we sort of cut around the invisible girl in a weird way, and the Lana and Clark story became the focus of the episode," Miles Millar notes. "I think we have two of the best scenes of the first season in that episode — the near-kiss and the scene at sunset. It really turned out much better than we thought it was going to — we really downplayed the crime story, and played up the romance and the drama between Clark and Lana."

Co-executive producer Ken Horton recalls that 'Shimmer' is an example of an episode changing dramatically during the post-production process. Once the footage has been shot in Vancouver, it is sent down to Los Angeles, where the special effects, music, and live action are all melded together in the editing room. "It was incredibly ambitious doing a show about an invisible person," Horton explains. "When we first started to put it together, we laughed at it, because it was basically pots and pans flying around. That whole side of the story was bizarre.

Eventually we decided to reshoot a scene, which was a financial mistake, but

Opposite: Lex makes his plans.

DID YOU KNOW?

Cadmus Labs is one of the mainstays of the DC Comics universe. During the period of Superman's death after his battle with Doomsday, they created the current Superboy when trying to clone Superman's tissue.

creatively the best 'mistake' we made the entire year. We shot the scene between Clark and Lana in the loft where she comes up to see the sunset. What was supposed to happen was that they were between the camera and the window. We would look out the window, and the sun is beginning to set. Then the rest of the scene was supposed to take place between Clark and Lana, without us looking out the window, because we were creating the sunset from scratch as an effect, which was expensive. They had budgeted for two greenscreen shots, but in the end James Marshall, who was doing all our second unit filming then, shot it over their shoulders so we were seeing out the window the whole time. There were seventeen greenscreen shots! It cost somewhere in the neighborhood of $50,000 to put in the sunset, but it was *magnificent*. It was probably the finest moment Bill Millar, who was doing our effects, did for that season."

SMALLVILLE TORCH

Volume 50, Number 51

I'M BACK

I'm back from my brief stint on admin's blacklist. Censorship issues tenaciously, if tentatively, resolved, I'm here to get us back on track with all things true. I have a few new "rules" I am supposed to abide by. Keep things "light", "school-related", fun. Stay away from dark alleys and "tabloid" issues. (Sound a lot like 'be blond, be bland, be boring'?)

I assume this wrist slapping was intended to hush my hollering about paranormal events, mutants, and such. And so I say this: I promise you, my faithful *Torch* readers, I will not print anything in this paper that I cannot firmly back up. My business is journalism. I'm here to find out the facts, and that's what I am going to do. From here on out, I'm Chloe Sullivan, and I'm here to bring you the Truth.

By Chloe Sullivan

"There's an emotional power to that scene," Mark Verheiden agrees. "Clark wants to go for it, and then Whitney comes and tells him this terrible thing about his father, so he has to *not* go for it. It's a really aching and poignant scene." With such a dramatic scene, "it allowed us to pare down the crime story and beef up the story between Clark and Lana," Horton continues. "Then we created an end where Clark went up and looked through the telescope, and Lana was with Whitney, and he was by himself. In many ways, that defined their relationship, and how intensely passionate it was, and how effective you could still be in this day and age with unrequited love. You just ached for those people."

CLARK: I'm just glad that you and I are so close.

LANA: Me, too. That's the thing about Clark Kent. He's not always there when you want him, but he's always there when you need him.

Verheiden was equally taken with the scene where Lex explains the history of his watch. "I still remember walking into the editor's room, and Michael Green and I saw a cut of that," he says. "We were both giggling and elbowing each other because it was such a nice story, told so well by Michael Rosenbaum. You saw so many levels of his feelings for his mother and father, and his loss."

"D.J. Caruso did a fantastic job for us," Miles Millar concludes. "There was a great scene in the armory with the mace coming into Clark's face. D. J. is a powerhouse!" ▪

SMALLVILLE MUSIC

'S.O.S.' by The Vigilantes of Love
'Galaxy' by The Vigilantes of Love
'When I'm With You'
  by Simple Plan
'Evolution Revolution Love'
  by Tricky
'If I Go' by Thrift Store Halo
'Blend' by Something Else
'Poor Misguided Fool'
  by Starsailor
'Caught In the Sun'
  by Course of Nature

HUG

WRITTEN BY: Doris Egan
DIRECTED BY: Chris Long

GUEST STARS: Kelly Brook (Victoria Hardwick), R. Nelson Brown (Lex's Doctor), Rick Peters (Bob Rickman), Gregory Sporleder (Kyle Tippet)

During a ride in the woods, Lana's horse is spooked and she is thrown. Local recluse Kyle Tippet comes to her aid, but Lana isn't sure if he was trying to harm or help her. Tippet's former sales partner Bob Rickman has recently arrived in Smallville, keen to open a new pesticide plant. With a handshake, Rickman is able to bend people's wills and make them do what he wants, leaving them with no memory of what happened afterward. To everyone's surprise, he is able to persuade Jonathan Kent to sell the farm. Rickman and Tippet have the same gift, and Rickman uses Whitney's anger at Tippet over the Lana incident to make him attack his former partner. Clark manages to stop Whitney, but Whitney believes that the recluse attacked him. Tippet demonstrates his power to Clark and Chloe, making her kiss Clark passionately. Rickman uses his power to send Lex after Clark and Tippet, and he also attacks them with a machine gun. Clark is able to save their lives, and luckily Lex has no memory of the attack once it's over. Rickman and Tippet use their power against each other, with Kyle the victor. Lex's lawyers manage to break the contract Jonathan signed, leaving the farm back in the Kents' hands.

LANA: What do you want to do?
CLARK: I'm not sure. Just as long as it doesn't involve putting on a suit and doing a lot of flying.

"Our show is interesting," Kristin Kreuk says with a smile. "It keeps you on your toes." Kristin has keen memories of the day when she, Tom Welling and Allison Mack went out on horseback to shoot the opening scenes of 'Hug'. Although Kristin's stunt double did a lot of her riding in scenes prior to this, notably when Lana is approaching the stable before her first meeting with Lex in 'Metamorphosis', Kristin herself was riding for this scene. Neither of her co-stars was as proficient as she was on horseback.

"It was a funny, funny day," she recalls. "We were on a track, and we had to position the horses so that we could all be on camera. Mine was on the inside, then Allison's, then Tom's. But the two of them just couldn't control their horses! It was a bit stressful, and Allison almost ran me over with her horse!"

'Hug' was the last episode to be filmed in 2001 before the cast and crew headed home for a well-deserved Christmas break, after five very intense months of shooting the early part of the first season. "Everyone was tired, and waiting to go home and go on vacation," Miles Millar points out. "It had been such a difficult few months. 'Hug' is very solid and very enjoyable, but it's not one of my favorites of the season. It had really good

Opposite: Lex and Bob Rickman.

potential, but it wasn't quite realized. It could have been even better."

Having said that, Millar notes that there were a great many positive points about the episode. "It was a more adult-focused show," he says. "I think the relationship between Kyle and Rickman plays on the Lex and Clark relationship, and really parallels that. Greg Sporleder, who played the hermit in the woods, is someone I really like and had worked with before."

LEX: You think I don't see the way your parents look at me? The way half the town looks at me? You're no different. Friendship's a fairy tale, Clark. Respect and fear are the best you can hope for.

The final scene between Lex and Clark, where Lex says, "Trust me, Clark. Our friendship is going to be the stuff of legends," was originally scripted to appear at the end of 'Metamorphosis'. "We took those lines, which we had always wanted to use, and put them at the end of this episode," Millar explains. "It paid off in that way. It's got a good

Below: Lex with the model of Rickman's proposed pesticide plant.

vibe and cool visual effects."

Michael Rosenbaum was pleased that 'Hug' gave him the first opportunity to show what Lex's reaction would be like if he discovered the truth about Clark. "When you do the same character over and over, week in and week out, you're just looking for that one moment where you can be different," he comments. "It's good to just show an edge, show something you haven't shown before!"

The episode also demonstrates the depth of Chloe's feelings for Clark. "I think they're trying to get Chloe and Clark to kiss once every season," Allison Mack jokes. "Somewhere slyly, once a year." ■

SMALLVILLE MUSIC

'Into the Lavender' by Rubyhorse
'Have a Nice Day' by
    Stereophonics
'Mistaken I.D.' by Citizen Cope
'Slow Down' by Wayne
'Into You' by Jennifer Knapp

Smallville ♦ Ledger

* * * Volume 64, Number 3 * * *

RICKMAN FOUND DEAD
Probable Suicide

Deputies from the Lowell County Sheriff's Office were called to B.B. Davenport's Route 7 auto repair shop on the desolate outskirts of town in response to an anonymous phone tip. There, they found the body of entrepreneur Bob Rickman lying outside the shop, dead from a gunshot wound to the head. No witnesses have come forward yet, but investigators have determined that the fatal injury was self-inflicted.

As previously reported in the Ledger, Rickman was visiting Smallville to pave the way for the construction of a pesticide plant in town. He had met considerable opposition from residents and authorities, who were well aware of the detrimental effects on the environment of Rickman's other plants. Rickman's primary focus had been on land owned for decades by the Kent family. Surprisingly, Jonathan Kent had signed away the heirloom plot with little hesitation, but later changed his mind and filed a lawsuit to challenge the contract.

Members of the Metropolis Police Department speculate that Rickman was frightened by their growing investigation into the mysterious death of Paul Hendrix, an agent for the Center For Environmental Protection. Documents found in Hendrix's office indicate that Rickman was under scrutiny by the center for past offenses, and the authorities were preparing to question Rickman as a suspect. Combined with the potential failure of Rickman's Smallville expansion attempt, the impending murder inquiry may have pushed Rickman to take his own life.

By Christopher James Beppo

LEECH

WRITTEN BY: Tim Schlattmann
DIRECTED BY: Greg Beeman

GUEST STARS: Kelly Brook (Victoria Hardwick), Tom O'Brien (Roger Nixon), Shawn Ashmore (Eric Summers), Kevin McNulty (Mr. Summers), Sarah-Jane Redmond (Nell Potter), William Samples (Sir Harry Hardwick), P. Lynn Johnson (Mrs. Summers), Mitchell Kosterman (Sheriff Ethan)

A school field trip ends badly when Clark and classmate Eric Summers are hit by lightning as Eric clutches some meteor rock. Somehow, Clark's powers are transferred to Eric. As Clark starts to come to terms with being a normal teenager, Eric allows the power to go to his head, first attacking his classmates, and then his parents. When Clark tries to stop Eric, he is badly injured. Despite this, Clark knows that it is his responsibility to bring Eric under control.

Clark is confronted by Lex, who is convinced by Roger Nixon's investigations that Clark must have been hit by his Porsche on the bridge, but when he sees Clark's injuries, he realizes that he must have been wrong. Clark and Eric fight, and a second jolt of electricity returns Clark's powers to him.

Lex and Lionel have been working together against Victoria and her father, Sir Harry Hardwick, planting false information in Lex's computer. As a result of its financial instability, the Luthors are able to buy Hardwick Industries. Nixon shows Lex evidence that Lionel and Victoria were also lovers. Lana learns that her Aunt Nell plans to sell her florist's shop, which means that the Talon cinema where her parents met will also be sold.

VICTORIA: We could have been great together.
LEX: I plan on being great all by myself.

'Leech' was a baptism of fire for new physical effects supervisor Mike Walls, who came on board *Smallville* just before the end of 2001. "I started a week-and-a-half before Christmas, and for that time I prepped an explosion that I knew was going to happen after Christmas," he recalls. "I waited around for a script, but nothing came, and when we came back after Christmas, we had an outline. Halfway through shooting the episode, the end sequence of 'Leech' became this monster that grew into itself. At that point, I turned to my assistant and said, 'Holy crap! We're in trouble here — this is way bigger than we ever imagined.' And from that point on, it's never stopped!"

When the writers and producers are devising ideas for *Smallville*, they often begin with the simple question, 'What if?' The questions, 'What if someone had a crush on Lana, and acted on that obsession?' and 'What if someone found out Clark's secret?' had been at the heart of 'Metamorphosis' and 'Rogue', and now the writers asked themselves, 'What if someone else had Clark's powers?' "I like the 'What if?' episodes," Miles Millar

Opposite: Clark says goodbye to Lana as he goes to face Eric.

explains, "because they usually turn out to be really good. They go right to Clark and his problem."

Greg Beeman also thinks that this episode answers the question, 'What if bad parents had found Clark?' "In 'Leech', Clark's powers are in a kid who has a bad father, and he goes bad," he says. "So Clark still has to be a hero, just as much as if Eric was a villain. The parent made a difference. I love the episodes where we explore the theme of parenting."

JONATHAN: Seeing how destructive Eric got, it just reminds me of how special you really are.

CLARK: That's because Eric didn't get my two strongest gifts: you and Mom.

Miles Millar describes 'Leech' as "the last big episode for the first season. The studio had been very generous with us for the first twelve episodes, but when we started the back nine episodes, they really came down on us. But for 'Leech', we had lots of money to spend, and I think the visual effects are fantastic. We really lucked out with Shawn Ashmore as well, who went on to star in the *X-Men* films. I loved the scene where he throws Clark around in the school parking lot."

Below: Clark vs Eric.

"He was great," Greg Beeman agrees. "He was perfect for that role. He actually stood on the edge of that bridge, on the edge of a 400-foot precipice. He was wired in, and we did the wire removal digitally, but we couldn't have gotten that shot where the camera twirls up around him."

The final question of the episode was how Clark would cope without his powers. "I loved that," Greg Beeman says. "I fought to get more of that in. I went to Al and Miles and said that I wanted to see the basketball game, and Clark gets hit in the nose. I wanted to see him get hurt and fall down. I wanted him to lose the basketball game *and* have the greatest day of his life, because he's not holding back." ∎

Smallville Ledger

* * * Volume 64, Number 4 * * *

SUPERBOY TURNS SUPERPSYCHO!

An unexplainable event occurred recently, and those who witnessed it are still trying to figure out how it happened. After watching a thief steal a purse from a female high school student, Eric Summers came to the aid of one of his classmates and retrieved the bag that contained a laptop computer.

Not only did Summers stop the attacker and save the computer, but he hurled the man at least thirty feet into the air! Defying all the principles of physics, the purse snatcher flew 30 feet — powered only by Summers' incredible strength. How did young Mr. Summers do that? I don't know, and I'm the student he helped. In fact, I typed this article on the laptop he saved.

But apparently, Summers doesn't plan to use his newfound powers solely for good. Yesterday, at Smallville High School, he got involved in a fight with a fellow student. In an uncontrollable rage, he flung a truck clear across the parking lot! He then launched two classmates at least 20 feet.

Last night, deputies responded to an emergency call from the troubled youth's parents. After law enforcement officials arrived at the scene, Summers overturned one of their cars and threw another through the roof of his parents' house, to the amazement of onlookers.

Authorities later found Summers unconscious near Rockway Dam, inexplicably electrocuted. He was rushed to Smallville Medical Center for treatment. According to hospital officials, medical experts from S.T.A.R. Labs have already arrived at the facility to study this incredible phenomenon. It was not clear at press time whether charges will be filed against Summers for the mayhem he caused.

By Chloe Sullivan

KINETIC

WRITTEN BY: Philip Levens
DIRECTED BY: Robert Singer

GUEST STARS: David Lovgren (Derek Fox), Kavan Smith (Wade Mahaney), David Coles (Scott Bowman), Sarah-Jane Redmond (Nell Potter)

Chloe's interview with Lex is curtailed when three robbers phase through the mansion walls and attack her and Clark, sending Chloe flying through a window. Lex refuses to report the robbery since he has lost a disc of confidential information relating to his misappropriation of LutherCorp funds, which the robbers offer to sell back to him. They are three former Smallville High students who use meteor rock ink tattoos to allow themselves to move through solid objects. When Whitney loses his scholarship and becomes disillusioned with his future prospects, he is seduced by the trio's easy lifestyle. They need new recruits, as the meteor rock tattoos' effects diminish each time they are applied. When they meet Lex, Clark interrupts and recognizes Whitney, who then goes to Lana for help. Clark and Whitney then recover Lex's disc and battle the trio, whose leader, Wade, doesn't realize that he is no longer able to phase, and is crushed by a car.

Meanwhile, Lex buys the Talon from Nell and is going to turn it into a parking structure, but Lana persuades him to make it a coffee shop when she produces a solid business plan.

CLARK: Sometimes I just wish I could leave this town and get away from the meteor rocks.

JONATHAN: Hey, hey. I'm sure that you will. You'll get that chance. But running away is not gonna solve anything.

"'Kinetic' is where the hammer came down budgetarily," Greg Beeman comments. "It was unfortunate, because it was a really great script. I loved it when I read it. It was really dark. There was some really cool stuff — these guys were walking through walls, and we were following them. There was a great scene where, in order to steal the merchandise inside the safe, one guy had to stand in the doorway and be used as a portal, and the others would throw all the stuff through him. But the hammer came down — it had to happen — and that episode got caught in the wringer."

Miles Millar also believes that 'Kinetic' is not as successful as some episodes "because there was no emotional context to what these guys were doing. We've had this problem a couple of times. Whenever we go to stories about guys who want money and use kryptonite deliberately to get it, it doesn't work. They're just after money. Our episodes work really well when we have a kid who gets a power, or a villain has some sort of emotional problem and their power reflects it. 'Leech' is about a kid who's bullied and

Opposite: Clark temporarily on his knees.

KINETIC

DID YOU KNOW?

The athletes are able to vibrate their molecules through solid objects — something they have in common with the DC Comics continuity version of the Flash, the Fastest Man Alive.

picked on and gets all the power he needs. Instead of being a hero about it, he exploits it. But in 'Kinetic', we have three villains who use kryptonite to make money. Who cares?"

The episode turns the focus clearly onto Whitney, and Eric Johnson was delighted at the opportunities it gave him. "I learned more than on any other episode," he says. "It was just a different way of thinking about what I was doing. I had to do a particular job and be very sure of what I was doing. I had more responsibility. When you have one scene, and you're in the background giving a dirty look, there's not a lot you have to put into it. But when you're the storyline, there's more."

However, it meant that Clark wasn't at the center of the story. "At one stage, we thought that since the show was called *Smallville*, we could have our other main characters — like Whitney or Lana — driving the A-story. It's not necessarily a Clark show," writer Philip Levens recalls. "Later on we backed away from that, but in the first year of any show, you're finding out what the show is, and we realized that it *is* the Clark Kent show. It has to be about Clark. So we redirected it after that."

Even if the budget was curtailed to a certain extent, 'Kinetic' was still a big show. "We had to cable every single car in the set at the end of the episode," physical effects supervisor Mike Walls points out. "There were probably about seventy-five cars up there. I had two guys in on a Sunday cabling them off, just so that the actors could work around them, because they were sitting precariously on these stacks of cars."

The episode begins with the attack on the Luthor mansion, and Chloe's traumatic fall. "It's fun to see people have the kind of enthusiasm that Kristin and Allison have," Walls says. "They just have no hesitation whatsoever — they just jump up and do it."

"Allison had a stunt double, Kathy Hubble, who was quite a good double for her,

Smallville 🐓 Ledger

* * * Volume 64, Number 5 * * *

LUTHOR ACQUIRES TALON PROPERTY

Smallville multimillionaire Lex Luthor has bought the Talon theater building on Main St. from owner Nell Potter for an undisclosed amount. The Talon, once the town's only movie house, closed last month, no longer able to compete in the multiplex-mania market. "Downtown Smallville is growing, and parking continues to be a problem. I'm considering building a parking structure for Smallville's downtown tenants and their customers," cited Luthor when asked about his plans for the historic property.

By Gena McGuiness

Opposite: Pete visits Chloe in hospital.

70 SMALLVILLE : SEASON 1

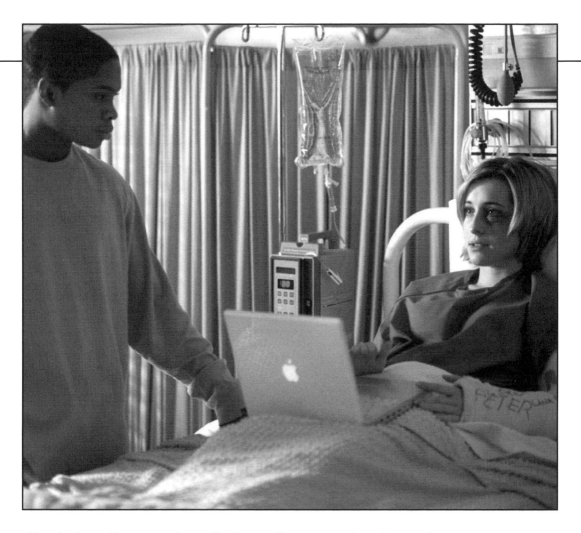

although a bit smaller," Lauro Chartrand explains. "Allison was gung-ho to do as much as she could, and to her credit, she did a lot of the hanging outside the building. Kathy went through the window — there was no way I could put Allison into that — then I had Allison cabled off, and we shot out the window and saw her hanging there over nothingness.

LEX: Clark, you can't save the world. All you'll end up with is a Messiah complex and a lot of enemies.

CLARK: I saved you, didn't I? That turned out all right.

"There was no CGI [computer generated imagery] involved there, and she did a great job. Then we pulled her in and hung Kathy out the window, and she fell about fifty feet to the ground." ■

SMALLVILLE MUSIC

'Set It Off' by P.O.D.
'New World Order' by Onesidezero
'I A.M.' by Beautiful Creatures
'Perfect Memory' by Remy Zero

ZERO

WRITTEN BY: Mark Verheiden
STORY BY: Alfred Gough & Miles Millar
DIRECTED BY: Michael Katleman

GUEST STARS: Cameron Dye (Sam Phelan), Corin Nemec (Jude Royce), Judy Tylor (Amanda Rothman), Mitchell Kosterman (Sheriff Ethan), Eric Breker (Amanda's Brother)

As Lana prepares to reopen the Talon, Lex's past catches up with him. Some years earlier he was involved in an incident at Club Zero in Metropolis, which resulted in the death of Jude Royce, the fiancé of Lex's friend Amanda, at the hands of the nightclub bouncer, Max. But somehow Jude has turned up in Smallville, leading to Max's death, an attack on a supplier at the Talon, and a chemical spillage at the Kent farm, for which Lex is held responsible. Despite Lex's attempts to keep him out of it, Clark investigates, and when Lex disappears, he tracks his friend down to the deserted Club Zero, where he is being held hostage by Amanda's brother, who is convinced that Lex, not Max, was responsible for Jude's death. Lex tells Amanda's brother that Amanda herself pulled the trigger, and Lex was trying to protect her. He refuses to believe Lex, but Clark arrives in the nick of time and saves his friend.

Meanwhile, Chloe is assigned to write a biography of Clark for a school project, but when she discovers that Clark was the only adoptee from Metropolis United Charities, she promises him she'll drop the investigation. However, she still keeps her files.

AMANDA: Zero consequences. That's quite a promise.
LEX: Only if it's kept.

"'Zero' was the start of a really good run," Miles Millar maintains, "I think we had really found our stride. We were getting into Lex's story, and playing with the structure of the story. That worked really well. Michael Katleman was the perfect director for the perfect script in terms of his directing style. He's very kinetic and very energetic with his camera work, which we don't tend to do on *Smallville*, but it worked really well for this episode."

"It was very dark," writer Mark Verheiden recalls, "and again, very interesting to work on." It was the first episode to use the idea of various narrators describing the same event, a technique most notably used in the Japanese film *Rashomon*. "We really wanted to try to do that sort of *Rashomon* idea, where you see the same event through different perspectives," Verheiden continues. "I like the idea that at the end of that episode, I don't think you really know if Lex killed Jude or not. You're left wondering. His story is that he didn't, but by then we've seen three or four unreliable narrators tell different versions of this event."

Verheiden himself doesn't believe Lex pulled the trigger. "I don't think he was that far gone — although I do think he brought Amanda in to see what Jude was up to. All of that was true, but I don't think he'd got to the point where he was going to kill anyone — yet."

Opposite: Lex realizes his past is catching up with him.

After an episode focused on Whitney's redemption, Lex took center stage in a tale that "gave Michael a real chance to stretch himself," Miles Millar says. The crew were very impressed with Rosenbaum's stamina in the grueling scenes. "It was very difficult to deal with the logistics of having somebody upside down for an entire episode," physical effects supervisor Mike Walls notes. "We had to be able to get him in and out of that position very quickly for each take. Michael was amazing — he was able to hold himself together for up to four or five minutes, which is a very long time to be upside down!" Rosenbaum himself remembers it well: "I like being challenged. I was kidnapped and held upside down, and my face was *this* big... all the blood and the veins [standing out], it was great!"

CLARK: So you took the fall and everything was covered up. Is that really what happened? Is it the truth?

LEX: The truth is, I'd do anything to protect my friends.

The final scene, where Lex goes over the balcony in the straitjacket, was a challenge for the young stuntman who doubled for Michael Rosenbaum. "Timing was the big issue," Lauro Chartrand explains. "It's a tough gag, falling backward with everything tied up, and he just froze. He had to initiate the move so the effects guys could blow the

Below: Lex tries to keep Clark and Lana out of his affairs.

glass on the fish tank. He started to move, but thought they weren't going to blow it in time, so he stopped. He didn't really commit, and with stunts and effects, you have to put your life in their hands, then forget about it and trust that it will happen."

"He did the lunge, but stopped at the last instant. Too late — they blew the glass. He stayed up there while all the glass came down! That was a huge reset to do it all again. It took all day to shoot that one little piece," Mike Walls recalls. "It was the first time that I had seen Clark time. We had Clark running in, pushing a sofa underneath the fish tank as Lex came through the tank and was landing. The logistics of that shot were incredible."

"I love 'Zero'," Greg Beeman enthuses. "In some ways I'd like to do more episodes like that. What I love about this show is that in some ways it's the same episode every week, and in other ways it's different every week. The style is adaptable. 'Zero' was a very adult show, with a very dark, very graphic visual style. It's our first Lex episode, and I'm proud of it." ▪

SMALLVILLE TORCH

Volume 50, Number 55

AN OPEN LETTER TO SMALLVILLE HIGH STUDENTS

Dear Students of Smallville High,

This week, we celebrated the grand reopening of the Talon Movie Theater and Coffee House. I wish to express my deep gratitude to a few individuals, without whom this event would not have succeeded.

First and foremost, thanks to Lex Luthor for his financial backing of the remodeling and reopening. I appreciate his prodding as well, which got me motivated to really pursue this endeavor.

I'd also like to thank Clark Kent for his unending support during times of leaks, breaks, and other unmentionable disasters.

Thanks to the dozens of carpenters, plumbers and electricians whose skill and time brought the Talon up to code and returned it to its original splendor.

And a big thanks to you, the students of Smallville High, for supporting me and the Talon at our opening night gala. I hope you will find it a nice place to "hang" and will come back often.

A few weeks ago, I talked about the importance of adding to our communities, and this week saw it in full force. I saw a community of heroes come to my aid and help me fulfill a dream. Thank you, Smallville.

As an expression of my appreciation, receive 15% off your order at the Talon when you present this issue.

Thank you again!

By Lana Lang

NICODEMUS

WRITTEN BY: Michael Green
STORY BY: Greg Walker
DIRECTED BY: James Marshall

GUEST STARS: Joe Morton (Dr. Steven Hamilton),
Hiro Kanagawa (Principal Kwan), Bill Mondy (James Beels)

Dr. Hamilton's research has led him to investigate the Nicodemus flower, whose pollen causes a total lack of inhibitions. His sample flower is stolen from his lab, and after the thief drives off the road, Jonathan Kent accidentally inhales the pollen when he goes to help. After behaving like a teenager, Jonathan suddenly becomes furious and drives into Smallville in a rage, fires a shotgun at Clark when his son tries to reason with him, and then collapses. As Jonathan's condition weakens, Lana and Chloe investigate the crash site, and Lana inhales the pollen, leading her to dump Whitney, attempt to seduce Clark, steal Lex's Porsche, and climb the local windmill. She too becomes angry, and collapses into Clark's arms. Lex tells Hamilton that he must find a cure. Chloe spotted Hamilton at the crash site, and she and Pete go to his lab, where Pete inhales the pollen, bringing all his anger at Lex to the surface. He goes to the mansion, where he finds Hamilton with Lex. Clark intervenes in time to stop Pete from killing Lex, as Hamilton escapes unnoticed. The Native American cure that the doctor has given Lex saves the lives of all but the original thief, who has already died, but leaves them with a blank space in their memories.

CHLOE: Clark, there are other girls out there that don't require crossing an emotional minefield.

CLARK: Yeah, but I can't just turn off my feelings for her.

CHLOE: You know, the choice is yours. You can either sit in your loft and play with your telescope, or move on.

"The *Dukes of Hazzard* theme on Jonathan Kent's radio was totally down to Ken Horton!" Miles Millar laughs. Horton is in charge of everything to do with post-production on the episodes, which often gives him leeway to make suggestions that can dramatically alter a scene. "He told us he'd done something, and we went and looked at it, and we really liked it. Nine out of ten times when he does that, we like it. On another episode, though, he had Lex playing Abba or something similar, and we said no — that was totally ridiculous!"

'Nicodemus' was "our first fun episode," Millar admits. "The show can be very earnest and very serious, and everyone wears their emotions on their sleeve. This episode, we had some fun and changed the personalities. It was James Marshall's first episode as director. He had shot that final scene in 'Shimmer' with Clark, Lana and Whitney, and from that scene we got him approved by the network."

Opposite: Lana Lang, seductive temptress.

"James Marshall is fantastic and has an incredible vision," Mike Walls notes. "But to get there is painstaking. He's meticulous in everything that he does. He wants to have it all, and wants it all available to him in any way possible. And it always turns out fantastic."

"That was James Marshall's break," Greg Beeman adds. "He got a great performance out of Kristin Kreuk. 'Nicodemus' was our first big Lana episode, but it has a little bit of everything. It's got strong Clark/Lana stuff, with naughty Lana, and Kristin showing a different side of herself."

Although it wasn't Kristin who stripped down to her underwear for the swimming sequence, it was her on the windmill. "She really impressed me," Lauro Chartrand recalls. "That was the first time that we got her into any stunts. She's so quiet and hard to read, and hadn't really had a whole bunch of action up till then. I was out there coaching her, and said that she only needed to go ten rungs or so, but she ran right to the top of the tower. We put her on cables, and we had her fall from the top of it, forty feet in the air."

"That was probably the most gutsy move I've ever seen from an actor," Mike Walls adds. "She had no hesitation whatsoever. Up until that point, she'd just been there as

Smallville ❦ Ledger

* * * Volume 64, Number 7 * * *

STRANGE FLU HITS SMALLVILLE
Four People Lapse Into Comas

... According to attending physician Dr. Kenneth Ruddzehn, "These were such unusual cases. We just didn't know what we had on our hands. Initially when a patient is brought into the hospital we try to rule out certain conditions in order to form a diagnosis. We ruled out all known bacterial or viral infections. All chem panels were normal. Except for the high fever, which didn't react to any of our usual treatments, I couldn't discern the problem. This proved to be very frustrating."

Dr. Ruddzehn then tried to make some sort of connection among the victims. "We know Kent came in contact with Beels, so initially I thought it could have been airborne, but Kent's wife and son didn't contract the illness, and no one on the medical staff who treated the two men became sick either." To add to the conundrum, the fevers broke immediately, and all three patients awoke from their comas. "I'm grateful the three appear to be cured. I only wish Mr. Beels could have been saved."

By Kathy Romita

Opposite: Clark and Chloe discuss the change in Lana.

the girl that Clark pines for, but she definitely let go in that episode."

Someone else who got a chance to let go in the episode, and do some of his own stunt work, was John Schneider. "Anything to do with his character he gets angry if you don't let him do it," Mike Walls notes. "He is probably better than most stunt guys that I've ever seen drive."

LANA: I know you want me, Clark. Stop holding back. Come on. You're not made of steel. Or are you?

"That was such a bonus," Lauro Chartrand says, "because we could let him do a lot of his stunt driving, as long as it didn't involve crashing. If it was sliding, we'd tell him to go for it. We'd give him some rehearsals in an open space, so I was confident he was on the money — which, of course, with all the driving he did on *The Dukes of Hazzard*, he was sharp as a tack. He would always spice it up when we rolled the cameras. In this episode, he wanted to holler out as he's sliding round the corner, but we'd already established that the window was rolled up, so the script supervisor said he couldn't have it rolled down. John responded by opening the door as he was doing the ninety degree slide around the corner!"

Sam Jones III enjoyed Pete's flower-induced attack on Lex. "I had an awesome time on that episode," he recalls. "I was just able to switch it up. Pete's usually so innocent and happy-go-lucky, but just being able to get a little bit of a dark side was really fun."

"I really liked 'Nicodemus' because it was an ensemble show," Annette O'Toole concludes. "Everyone got a shot at something. There was a storyline for everybody and they were all good." ▪

'Good Ol' Boys' (theme song
  from *The Dukes of Hazzard*)
  by Waylon Jennings
'I Will Make U Cry'
  by Nelly Furtado
'Destiny' by Zero 7
'I Have Seen' by Zero 7
'Supernatural' by Divine Right
'Sadie Hawkins Dance' by Relient K.
'Big Day' by Puracane
'Love Sweet Love'
  by Josh Clayton-Felt
'Saturday Night's Alright'
  by Hal Lovejoy
'Beautiful Day' by U2

STRAY

WRITTEN BY: Philip Levens
DIRECTED BY: Paul Shapiro

GUEST STARS: Ryan Kelley (Ryan James), Brandy Ledford (Ryan's Stepmom), John Glover (Lionel Luthor), Jim Shield (Ryan's Stepdad), Courtney Kramer (Skye)

Young Ryan James enters the Kents' lives when Martha hits him with her car as he races across a road. He was trying to escape from his stepfather and his new wife, who are using his ability to read minds in order to carry out a series of robberies. Everyone becomes fond of Clark's 'younger brother', and Ryan displays his powers when he warns Lana about a dishonest waitress, tells Clark about Chloe's hopes that he'll invite her to the Spring Formal, and the offer that Lex has received from his father to return to Metropolis. When Ryan's stepfather tracks him down, Ryan hides inside some garbage which is then thrown into a compactor, and Clark tears the side off the compactor in order to save him. Ryan then reads Martha's mind and discovers Clark's spaceship. Ryan's stepmother masquerades as a local social services official and takes Ryan from the Kents; at the same time his stepfather replaces Lex's chauffeur. They force Ryan to read Lex's mind for his safe combination before dumping Lex by the side of the road. Clark races after Ryan, who escapes from his stepfather into a bowling alley. Clark knocks Ryan's stepfather out before taking Ryan back to the farm, where he is shortly united with his aunt from Edge City. Lex, meanwhile, refuses to leave Smallville.

LIONEL: We don't need to play games, son.
LEX: Dad, games are all we've got.

"I adore Ryan Kelley," Annette O'Toole enthuses. "He's a wonderful kid." She's speaking on behalf of cast and crew, all of whom enjoyed working with the young actor who made his first appearance as Ryan James in 'Stray'. "Ryan Kelley was fantastic," Miles Millar agrees. "And he got on really well with Tom."

"That was a beautiful episode," Greg Beeman comments. "We cast the right kid with Ryan Kelley. He was so sympathetic, and very empathetic. It was a fun story, and one that depended on the writing. It was one of our first episodes with hardly any visual effects at all, other than the bowling ball at the end."

"It was one of the first episodes where people saw that *Smallville* could be about something different," writer Philip Levens notes. "It didn't have to be about beating up the kryptonite villain — there's no kryptonite in 'Stray' at all. Originally, we did have a kryptonite explanation for Ryan's powers, but then we decided to pull it and do it without."

"I always wanted to have a kid on the show," Miles Millar recalls. "It would be Clark and the kid together. We did a version in the outline stage where he was a bad seed — the Kents adopted the wrong kid." Levens elaborates: "Ryan was going to be a killer who

Opposite: Lex with the young 'stray', Ryan James.

escaped from a foster home. This little boy was sucked in." "The network hated that," Millar continues. "They wanted to see the kid, but they wanted us to have a nice kid. The kid still had telepathic powers in the bad seed version, so we just went the other way with it and made him very sympathetic. It worked really well."

Part of the success of 'Stray', Millar believes, is that it's another 'What if?' episode. "Once again, it was about Clark," he says. "What if he had been raised by the wrong people and his power had been exploited? It just mirrors Clark's life, and again we see that Clark really is who he is because of his parents."

The scene where Lex is thrown out of the limousine was deliberately designed to shock. Stunt coordinator Lauro Chartrand was asked to make sure it looked violent, while at the same time ensuring that it was safe. "It was the same young guy who doubled for Lex in 'Zero'," he recalls. "He did a great job in rehearsals, and did a great job on set. We were doing twenty miles an hour when he got tossed out. It was really

Opposite: Ryan, Lex, and Clark: three *Warrior Angel* fans.

Smallville ✦ Ledger

★ ★ ★ Volume 64, Number 8 ★ ★ ★

LOST BOY FINDS HIS WAY HOME

"We're happy to know he's with a loving family member and look forward to him coming back to visit," says Martha Kent of twelve-year-old Ryan. A few days ago, while driving Route 90, Kent literally ran into the lost boy when Ryan dashed out onto the road. Rushed to the hospital, Ryan suffered only minor cuts and bruises but claimed to have no memory other than his name. With no evidence of head injuries, doctors assessed his temporary memory lapse as traumatic shock. Unable to contact next of kin, hospital administrators and the Kents were in a quandary over what to do with the youngster. "We weren't going to let him stay in the sheriff's juvenile cell until Child Services could come for him," says Jonathan Kent, "so we brought him home with us."

By Gena McGuiness

violent, and looked really good. He scratched his head a little bit, but the medics touched it up with a Band-Aid and he was fine."

In fact, when the producers saw the dailies (the film shot on the previous day), they were concerned that it might be *too* violent. "You could hear his elbow pad hit the pavement at the same time as his head hit the pavement," Chartrand continues. "His head just scuffed the pavement, it wasn't a smack, but they thought that this noise was his head! The guy's timing was perfect, so it just makes you cringe."

LEX: Apparently, we're both big *Warrior Angel* fans.

CLARK: I didn't know you liked comic books.

LEX: A strange visitor from another planet who protects the weak. When I was young, he was my idol. Not to mention the fact he's bald.

Physical effects supervisor Mike Walls would like another chance to recreate Clark's rescue of Ryan. "It was very difficult to envision what they wanted to do and try to make it, practically, without buying a truck, or building something ourselves," he recalls. "We tried to do it practically, using an existing truck that we could rent, and the CG guys did an amazing job to make it look good, but now I'd fight to build it ourselves. Up till then I had always tried to do things the conventional way, but after that, we really dug around to find different options of ways for Clark to bend metal." ∎

SMALLVILLE MUSIC

'Free to Change Your Mind'
   by Regency Buck
'Lonely Day' by Phantom Planet
'Is It Love?' by Todd Thibaud
'Dragging Me Down'
   by Todd Thibaud
'You and I' by Micah Green
'Superman' by Five For Fighting

REAPER

WRITTEN BY: Cameron Litvack
DIRECTED BY: Terrence O'Hara

GUEST STARS: John Glover (Lionel Luthor), Jason Connery (Dominic Santori), Sheila Moore (Mrs. Sikes), Reynaldo Rosales (Tyler Randall)

While smothering his mother to save her from a painful death from cancer, Tyler Randall is interrupted and falls to his death from a hospital window. However, when meteor rock embedded in his body is removed during the autopsy, he returns to life — with the ability to turn anything organic to dust when he touches it. He joins Clark and Martha on their rounds helping old people, and returns to kill one of the patients, Mrs. Sikes. Clark saves Martha from Tyler's touch, and Tyler overhears a conversation about Whitney's dying father and goes to the hospital to put Mr. Fordman out of his misery. However, Clark has learned that Tyler's mother didn't die, and Tyler shakes his own hand in order to kill himself.

It takes Whitney time to come to terms with his father's illness, but eventually he visits him. Lex arranges for the Metropolis Sharks to come to Smallville so Whitney's father can see him play with them. Clark and Jonathan are at odds over their annual fishing trip, but eventually reconcile. Lionel sends his accountant Dominic to check Lex's books, but Lex sends him packing — though not before Dominic has questioned Jonathan about Lex's continuing investigation into the accident. Lex assures Jonathan he has now closed the book on the incident.

CLARK: Dad, what would you say if we could be sitting in a deluxe box next Sunday watching the Metropolis Sharks?
JONATHAN: I'd say the Milk River's changed quite a bit.

"'Reaper' is an episode about the world's nicest deadly guy," Greg Beeman comments. "Those ideas are incongruent: this guy is going around touching people and killing them, but he's a really nice guy whom we really like!"

"The episode went through several permutations before we settled on the final story," Mark Verheiden recalls. "Originally the bad guy was an escaped prisoner. That changed because we were trying for a more sympathetic villain, and an escaped prisoner feels like something that belongs in a different show. Even so, the antagonist does dark things, like killing his mother in the teaser [pre-credits sequence], so that sympathy was tough to elicit. When you have the death touch, that just takes you to a dark place."

Mike Walls remembers 'Reaper' as "a pretty straightforward episode. The guy coming out the window took all night to shoot, but otherwise that was one of the episodes that was pretty easy to deal with. It was not over the top in any way, shape or form, which was a good thing, because of what was coming up!"

Lauro Chartrand comments that "the guest star was a good guy, and pretty gung-ho

Opposite: Chloe discovers the grim truth about Tyler in the Torch offices.

to do the fights. In the hospital, there was a little fight scene, and that was all the actors, except for the part where Clark throws the guy out the door and across the hallway. We used our stunt guy on a cable for that. Tyler Randall wanted to do it, and I had to point out to him that if he cracked his head and *stayed* in the hospital, it wouldn't be a good thing for me, or for him!

"Most of the gags [effects or stunts] that Tyler did were pretty rough. There was an air ram gag where he was after Martha, and Clark sent him flying. I started the shot with the actor flying off of an apple box, and got some good energy out of him flying back into some boxes, and then put our stunt guy on an air ram and sent him across the room. With the high fall in the teaser, it was fifty feet, so we had a stunt guy in there to come out the window and do the whole thing."

LEX (TO CLARK): You have no idea how lucky you are. When my father dies, kings will come to his funeral, but when yours dies, his friends will come.

'Reaper' also saw Jason Connery's Dominic Santori underestimate Lex. "We first introduced Dominic in 'Hothead' with the idea that he was a rival that Lionel was grooming," Al Gough recalls. "This was at a time in the series when John Glover was still a guest star, and we weren't sure how often we would see him. As it became apparent to us that we would be able to get him on a more regular basis, we didn't have to rely on a middleman character. That being said, we love Jason, and didn't want to lose him altogether. We brought him back for 'Reaper', as a pawn in the ongoing Lex/Lionel game." ∎

Right: Lex and Clark talk about friendship.

SMALLVILLE TORCH

Volume 51, Number 57

GETTING TO KNOW YOU: ALEXANDER LUTHOR

Round two. Me and Luthor Jr. The first time I sat down to interview Mr. Luthor, I found myself swan diving out of his third story window before I had a chance to get him on tape. Mr. Luthor was kind enough to grant me another interview op now that my wounds have healed. This time around though, Lex got a little camera shy and also made me promise not to ask him about anything involving LuthorCorp. So there are no revelations about Level 3 here — I'm sorry to disappoint. But, I did get to learn a little more about the enigma that is Alexander (that's right) Luthor.

By Chloe Sullivan

CHLOE: Is Lex short for something?

LEX: Actually, it's Alexander.

CHLOE: After Alexander the Great?

LEX: I've heard that version before.

CHLOE: That's fitting in a kind of freaky way. Tell me about your childhood — what should I know about your parents?

LEX: As far as my father is concerned, feel free to call his office. They'll send you his official biography — I think they can send a CD-ROM version now.

CHLOE: And your mother?

LEX: My mom died when I was thirteen. Fortunately, a child is the sum of both parents. My mother was the one who taught me there are many ways to see the world.

CHLOE: You seem very fond of her.

LEX: I was, and I am.

CHLOE: Could you talk about your educational background?

LEX: Throw a dart at a map of Europe, I was probably there. I spent semesters in Gstaad, Vienna, Paris, eventually graduating from Oxford. My father insisted I have a well-rounded educational background.

CHLOE: Was it?

LEX: I can say "vodka gimlet" in six languages. That's a joke, of course. (pretends to look at a fake camera) Lex Luthor does not support underage drinking. (back to me) In truth, schools 'educate', but I've found that life experience is perhaps as important to a learned mind.

CHLOE: What are your ambitions?

LEX: When I was six, I made the mistake of saying "fireman" to my father. I've found that ambitions and goals can change with circumstance. For the first time, I feel like I have a home here in Smallville, true friends. If I have an ambition, it's to hold on to that.

CHLOE: That's very cool. Thank you, Mr. Luthor.

LEX: It's Lex to you, Ms. Sullivan.

SMALLVILLE MUSIC

'Sparkle' by Rubyhorse
'Friends & Family' by Trik Turner
'The Weight of My Words' by Kings of Convenience
'Falcor' by Firengine Red

DRONE

WRITTEN BY: Philip Levens
& Michael Green
DIRECTED BY: Michael Katleman

GUEST STARS: Marguerite Moreau (Cassandra Castle),
Simon Wong (Paul Chan), Shonda Farr (Sasha), Hiro
Kanagawa (Principal Kwan)

Opponents of Sasha Woodman in the upcoming class elections for class president have a habit of falling ill. When popular Paul Chan is the subject of a bee attack, Pete puts Clark forward as an alternative candidate. Sasha has been able to control swarms of bees after being stung by bees nesting in a meteor-infested crater. She uses them to attack Clark and Lana, then sends them after Martha Kent, but Clark is able to stop them, and the bees turn on Sasha. Chloe and Clark fall out when the *Torch* backs Paul Chan for president, but he eventually agrees that Paul was the right choice. Paul wins the election, and only Lana ever hears Clark's victory speech.

Meanwhile, sales at the Talon are dropping and Lex encourages Lana to be more aggressive. She discovers that the rival store has health violations, which she publicizes, resulting in more trade. Lex also has to deal with a persistent investigative journalist, Cassandra Castle from the *Metropolis Journal*, who promises to write a positive piece about him, but is actually writing a hatchet job. To prevent this, Lex arranges for her to be promoted, and she tells him that Lionel was behind her piece.

LEX: There's nothing wrong with a good fight. Just remember, the man of tomorrow is forged by his battles today.

"How do you make bees believable?" physical effects supervisor Mike Walls asks rhetorically about the special guest creatures on 'Drone'. "All the scenes with the bees hitting the window turned out way better than I thought they ever would. For that scene, the bees were made from puffed wheat, Styrofoam, and popcorn, just painted black and gold. We had two guys who did nothing but paint our bees black and gold for days on end. Their fingers still ache to this day, I'm sure! We probably made six or seven hundred gallons worth of bees. Then we just pounded them with air movers against the windows."

The episode was a challenge in many respects for the effects department. The garage itself was a 'build' — something constructed specifically for the episode — "and because we knew we were blowing it up at the end of the story, we had built it in such a fashion so that it would come apart nice and easy, and make it look really fantastic in the explosion," Walls notes. "That explosion is one of my favorites from the whole show — it was nice and huge, and did exactly what it was supposed to do. But to do all the practical stuff that had to be done inside the garage was challenging, to say the least. The honeycomb was very difficult, because it wasn't at all what I envisioned. It was totally

Opposite: Cassandra Castle's quarry: Lex Luthor.

different and bizarre, and it took a bit of thinking to make that work."

Not all the bees were made of puffed wheat: in several sequences, the swarm was inserted digitally. This could be tricky for the actors, as Kristin Kreuk explains: "We were in the Talon, and you can't have a real swarm of killer bees coming at you, so they're fake, and you're looking up and you're acting to nothing. Argh!! Killer bees! And there's nothing there..." However, the scene where Principal Kwan opens the door to find Felice covered in bees featured a real person — and genuine bees. "Believe it or not, that was real," Mike Walls says. "It was the beekeeper — I don't think anyone else was stupid enough to do it. We found a whole pile of bees, and the beekeeper put all these bees around his face inside the car. He had to open the door and fall out. He ended up getting stung about twenty-five to thirty times. That day was just insane, but it looked better than it ever would have looked if we had done it with computer imagery."

Both Miles Millar and Greg Beeman are surprised at the less than positive reaction that the episode got from some fans. "It's interesting, because we always find that the rabid fans hate the high school episodes," Millar says, "but the teen audience who watch the show love them. I'm actually a big fan of the teen shows, and I thought 'Drone' was really successful. It's a really cool, interesting, inventive teen story." "What I like about 'Drone' is that it was very high school-based," Greg Beeman agrees. "We added a little bit more bubble gummy colors to our color pallet."

SMALLVILLE TORCH

Volume 51, Number 59

PAUL FOR PREZ
Endorsement of One

In recent weeks, Pete Ross has written extensively about the importance of our representative student government actually being representative. We are now in the midst of our annual glorified popularity contest — the Student Government Elections. It's my turn to endorse a candidate. Principal Kwan won't allow the *Torch* to make an official endorsement. So this one is mine and mine alone.

Every year since we've been in the third grade, the 'popular' students entered the school elections races. They usually won. Then when it came time to actually be a leader, they found themselves in over their heads, and nothing significant for the students ever got accomplished. This year is different, however. We have a candidate who has integrity, commitment, and maturity. Paul Chan wants to be president because he wants to make our experience here a little better. Show your commitment to your school. Vote for Paul Chan. And find yourself represented.

By Chloe Sullivan

Opposite: The explosive demise
of the swarm.

All the challenges are grist to the mill for line producer Bob Hargrove, and 'Drone' is a good example of the balance that *Smallville* has to achieve each week. "The scripts always come in large, and then we have to get to a position where we can execute them without sacrificing a good product," he explains. "A lot of series have one element that they deal with — either action or drama or special effects. We deal with all three. As far as I'm concerned this show is about our characters. People watch this show to see these characters. That's all well and good, but we also have action. We blow things up, we drop things, we create super hero moments which are sometimes difficult to achieve.

CHLOE: I just want to know what you stand for.
CLARK: I stand for truth, justice, and... other stuff.

"Then we have our visual effects. We have these three elements that we have to put together, and we basically have eight days of principal photography and two days of second unit to do it. The biggest challenge on this show is to do that well, every week." ∎

CRUSH

WRITTEN BY: Philip Levens
& Alfred Gough & Miles Millar
DIRECTED BY: James Marshall

GUEST STARS: John Glover (Lionel Luthor), Hiro Kanagawa
(Principal Kwan), Donna Bullock (Pamela Jenkins), Adam
Brody (Justin Gaines), Kevan Ohtsji (Danny Kwan)

DID YOU KNOW?

Adam Brody has since gone on
to play Seth Cohen, one of the
lead characters in the Fox
series *The O.C.*.

Talented artist Justin Gaines has lost the use of his hands after an accident, but is able to move things through telekinesis. After arranging for the mutilation of the surgeon he holds responsible for his lack of progress, he returns to Smallville, bent on revenge on the driver of the car who injured him. With Chloe's unwitting help, he discovers that the license plate belongs to Principal Kwan, and he kills Kwan by crushing him to death with his own car. However, Kwan wasn't at the wheel on the relevant night — it was his son, Danny. Although Clark has been trying to persuade Chloe that Justin is not the nice guy she thinks he is, she has not listened, until she finally finds evidence. Justin turns on Chloe, but Clark saves her.

Lex's old nanny Pamela tracks him down. Lex believes she abandoned him after his mother's death, but Pamela eventually reveals that Lionel threw her out. Now she is dying of cancer and wants Lex's forgiveness. When he learns the truth, Lex reconciles with her before her death.

Meanwhile, just as Lana is about to tell Whitney that it is over between them, Whitney's father dies.

CLARK: Chloe, why are you being so hypersensitive?
CHLOE: You know, most men are from Mars, Clark, but you're from some distant galaxy that I've never even heard of.

"I get killed off quite a lot," Hiro Kanagawa says in a very matter of fact tone. "It wasn't a complete surprise. Either Principal Kwan was going to develop, or, since he had been in peril so many times, it seemed quite obvious that he was targeted to be killed off. I've had some spectacular 'deaths' in my career, and I guess that Principal Kwan went in a fittingly spectacular way!"

"Al and I always thought that it's good to kill off regular characters," Miles Millar explains, "because viewers don't expect it. They're surprised when you do it, and then they basically never know what to expect. We were quite big fans of the series *Millennium*, and they had an episode where they killed off one of the leads. It was so shocking, and it's a really good way to keep everyone on their toes."

"'Crush' was the first show that I was the production designer for," Rob Maier notes, "I remember that we squashed Principal Kwan at a house in North Vancouver." Mike Walls adds, "We wanted the car to go right into the back, where we had built a fake back wall to the garage, and it would look like Hiro was pinned completely."

"There was a stunt guy strapped to the hood of the car," Lauro Chartrand explains,

Opposite: Clark must face the telekinetic Justin Gaines.

"and we cabled off the car and pulled it in so it could only go so far, then the stunt guy went off the hood and got squashed. Once he made contact with the wall, and the breakaway tool bench at the back, then we cut to a piece of Hiro going in and let him do his acting. Everyone was worried that it was going to be too gruesome!"

The episode closes with the funeral of Whitney's father. "I think that is the single most beautiful scene in the first season," Greg Beeman states. "It's beautiful and visually poetic." Miles Millar agrees: "I love that sequence in the rain. With the Eva Cassidy song, and Clark looking at Lana over the grave, and the rain falling, it was just really beautiful."

Appearances on a television show can be deceiving. "We manipulated the rain," Greg Beeman admits. "It was a bright, sunny day. I told the director of photography to make sure it was backlit. We would run in slow motion and use a ninety-degree shutter, and I knew it would be awesome. A lot of people get very rule-bound, and the rules say that you're not supposed to do rain when it's sunny — but it looked gorgeous. I kept saying that Ridley Scott would have done it!"

One of the most telling edits of that sequence shows Chloe's reaction as Clark looks

Below: Chloe falls for the wrong guy (again).

across at Lana at the funeral. "Our subtext became text," Greg Beeman says. "Chloe's interested in Clark — let's push that triangle. Of all our young cast, Allison was the most experienced. It was great in the cutting room — whenever you do a shot of her, she does something a little bit different, and it's always great. You end up with five takes and five different great choices. She was our 'go to' girl in season one — we could always go to Chloe, because she was always doing something interesting."

LEX: What's the problem?
CLARK: I've got these two amazing friends who both happen to be girls.
LEX: For argument's sake, let's call them Lana and Chloe.

"Once again, Chloe fell in love with the wrong guy!" Miles Millar concludes. "Those are always fun episodes. I really like 'Crush' — it's highly violent, with the doctor's hands caught in the elevator at the start, the really cool CG chainsaw, and bye-bye Principal Kwan. Chloe and Lana are really good too, and Adam Brody's distinctive voice suited his role." ■

SMALLVILLE MUSIC

'You and I' by Micah Green
'40 to 5' by Leave the World
'Nothing to Do' by Bottlefly
'Light In Your Eyes'
  by Louise Goffin
'2001 Spliff Odyssey'
  by The Thievery Corporation
'Time After Time' by Eva Cassidy

Smallville ⊙ Ledger
* * * Volume 64, Number 11 * * *

LUTHORCORP MIS OVERHAUL
Hackers Beware

LuthorCorp MIS director Will Soo has been hitting the caffeine pretty hard these days. Soo's been hard at work reconfiguring the LuthorCorp internal computer system into the most secure company system available…

"It's just pathetic to watch these amateurs try to get in. We had a little incident here a while ago when some British trick stole a username and password and read a couple of e-mails, and since then I've overhauled the whole joint. The user names have changed, and the passwords rotate at infrequent intervals. The personnel files and holdings cannot be accessed without our proprietary thumb-scanning software and peripherals, and the Indigo Charlie terminal — forget about it. Basically, my friend, no one is getting into this [expletive deleted]."

Mocking the many failed hacking attempts, Soo continued, "Yeah, guys, congratulations on right-clicking and hitting 'play'. If that were all it took to get Lionel Luthor's Swiss bank account numbers, I'd be a dead man."

By Mark Dee

OBSCURA

WRITTEN BY: Michael Green
& Mark Verheiden
STORY BY: Greg Walker
DIRECTED BY: Terrence O'Hara

GUEST STARS: Darrin Klimek (Deputy Gary Watts),
Robert Wisden (Gabe Sullivan), Tom O'Brien (Roger Nixon),
Joe Morton (Dr. Steven Hamilton), Aaron Douglas
(Deputy Birdego), Mitchell Kosterman (Sheriff Ethan)

DID YOU KNOW?

The sequences outside Watts' workshop were filmed at the P.N.E. in Vancouver — the funfair is a real Vancouver attraction, open throughout the summer.

Whitney and Lana's horse ride is interrupted by a gas explosion, which renders Lana unconscious. When she awakes, she starts having visions of Chloe being kidnapped, as if through the kidnapper's eyes. Chloe in fact has been kidnapped, and Lana is able to give Clark enough clues that he finds her buried in Chandlers Field and rescues her. Lana continues to get the visions, and they realize that one of the policemen at the scene of the explosion, Watts, is the culprit. He kidnaps Lana, but Clark tracks him down from Lana's visions, and Watts is killed in a gun battle with the police.

Meanwhile, journalist Roger Nixon's investigations into Lex's accident have revealed a crop duster who thinks he saw a spaceship land during the meteor shower. Lex investigates the field, much to the annoyance of Jonathan Kent, who is worried that Lex will find evidence of the ship. Jonathan tears up the check that Lex has just handed him in compensation for the lost herd (see 'Zero'). Dr. Hamilton finds an octagonal object of unearthly origin in the field, which in fact does come from Clark's ship. Roger Nixon starts to stalk Clark after he observes him using his powers.

Whitney finds his father's old war medals, and Clark asks Chloe to be his date for the Spring Formal.

JONATHAN: You're right, I got no real reason to doubt him. It's just something in my gut tells me I should.

CLARK: Lex isn't perfect, Dad. I know that. But slamming the door in his face over and over only helps turn him into exactly what you think he already is.

"'Obscura' was a really well-conceived show," Miles Millar recalls. "It's a true crime story but also has the kryptonite element — a bit like 'Hourglass', in a way — and it really set up the finale. On the page the concept was a bit hackneyed; it was a bit like the film *The Eyes of Laura Mars*, but it turned out really well. Terrence O'Hara delivered a really good show."

"I love horror movies, and 'Obscura' is a favorite for me," recalls Mark Verheiden. "It has two moments in it that I really love. One is when Chloe is buried alive by the psycho and Clark rips her out of the ground — she finally expresses all the pent up, romantic stuff she feels about him. Then when Lana was in jeopardy at the end, it was

Page 97 (following color section): Clark worries about Chloe's disappearance.

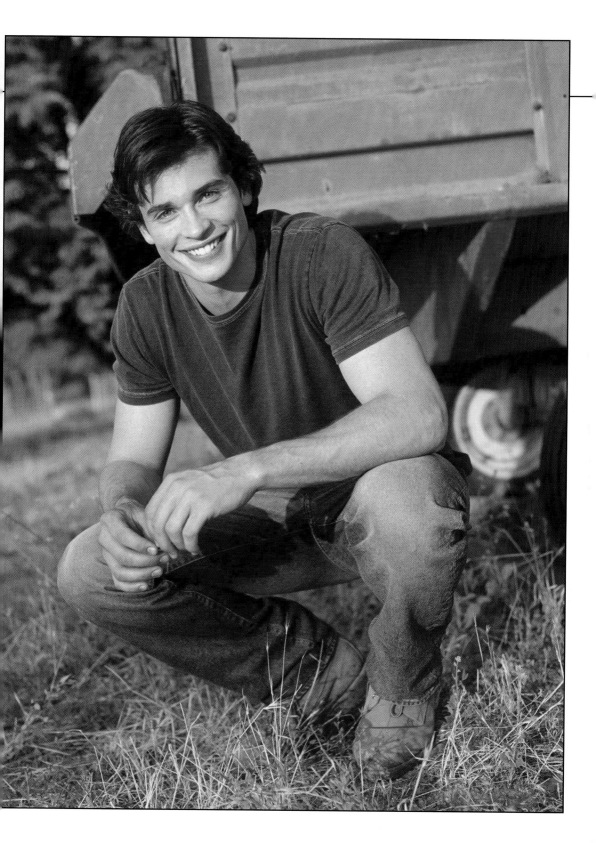

This painting, by the acclaimed comics artist
Alex Ross, was split across 4 special collectors'
covers of *TV Guide* in December 2001.

Above: Clark tries to figure out what Lana's visions mean.

done very effectively. You felt really afraid for her."

"When Tom pulled the coffin out of the ground, that was done in one shot," Mike Walls remembers. "I didn't think that would work, but we decided to go for it, and it was amazing how well it worked out. He reached his hand into a bunch of peat moss, and we had pre-designed the path for the crate to come up, which was on a wire system with five guys pulling it up from the other end. There's a lag where he changes position a little bit to keep pulling it out further, and that meant the guys were able to get a better grip and keep going — the lag wasn't supposed to be there but it worked out."

The opening sequence was one of the most visually impressive of the first season, with the camera swooping down over Lana and Whitney riding in the fields. "They were riding along Zero Avenue, not far from where the Kent farm is," production designer Rob Maier explains. "There's a stretch of Zero Avenue which is just picturesque. It's the road that runs right along the border — the field on the right is in the USA, and on the left is Canada, but it all looks so Kansas! Generally in the summer, it's just miles of corn, and as long as we don't show Mount Baker in the background, it's perfect."

"Bob Hargrove wanted to bring helicopters to *Smallville* — he was an old helicopter pilot from Vietnam — and sure enough we did, beginning with 'Obscura'," Greg

> **DID YOU KNOW?**
>
> The title comes from a 'camera obscura' — a device to enable artists to see things more clearly, that dates back to the third century B.C.. It literally means 'dark room' in Latin.

SMALLVILLE TORCH

Volume 51, Number 61

HIGH SCHOOL SUCKS
And Other Lies You Should Stop Telling Yourself

The other day I was in Spanish class. We had a substitute teacher. He did not speak any Spanish. But he was not dumb. Not even close. He was one of those wise old men with a funky twinkle in his eye. You know the type. He obviously wasn't going to teach us any Spanish, so he starts a conversation. He picks Spring Formal as the topic. One unnamed student — let's call her Bitter Election Loser, or Bitter for short — vomited out, "I will not go to the Spring Formal. This high school sucks. I just want to take the G.E.D. and move on to college to get away from all these drones."

Substitute Spanish teacher — did I mention he doesn't know how to speak Spanish? — chimes in, "Miss, boycotting school dances because high school sucks will leave you one day asking yourself, 'What happened to high school?' For surely if you keep up this attitude, you'll quickly feel the same way about the next stage of your life. And you will be sad. And you'll not be able to wait for the next stage to come, only to start the cycle all over again. High school sucks because that's exactly how you have chosen to experience it."

By Anonymous

'No Such Thing' by John Mayer
'Just Another' by Pete Yorn
'Two Stones In My Pocket'
  by Neil Halstead
'Piano Fire' by Sparklehorse
'Silent to the Dark'
  by Electric Soft Parade

Beeman recalls. "Bob and I are opposites, but we've always had a lot of respect for each other. We complement each other, and by this time we were starting to work on all cylinders together. I remember watching the teaser of 'Obscura' on-air, and realizing that this show was *huge*. We had a gas main blowing up, a huge fireball, and Kristin being blown in the air — unbelievably huge!"

"The script originally had a big fire," Mike Walls recalls, "but Terrence O'Hara, who's one of my favorite directors on the show, asked what I could give him. We ended up turning the scene into that big explosion, and they let me do what I wanted to do out there!"

Mark Verheiden also likes the emotional progression in the episode as everything builds toward the season finale. "Lex finds the key in the field, and Jonathan refuses the check when he realizes that Lex has been investigating again," he says. "But the horror story is pretty big in the episode. It's big because when you do a story where one of your main characters is kidnapped, that sucks all of the audience's attention. It's really hard to cut away to Lana cleaning up in the coffee shop when Chloe's been kidnapped! Everyone's concerned with that agenda, and it heats up the story pretty good." ∎

TEMPEST

WRITTEN BY: Alfred Gough
& Miles Millar
STORY BY: Philip Levens
DIRECTED BY: Greg Beeman

GUEST STARS: John Glover (Lionel Luthor), Tom O'Brien (Roger Nixon), Robert Wisden (Gabe Sullivan), Remy Zero (themselves)

SMALLVILLE **MUSIC**

'What Do I Have to Do?'
by Stabbing Westward
'Where This Love Goes'
by Sherri Young
'Everything' by Lifehouse
'Breathe' by Greenwheel
'Let Go' by Gigolo Aunts
'What We've Been Through'
by Paul Trudeau
'Save Me' by Remy Zero
(performed live)
'Perfect Memory'
by Remy Zero (performed live)

Lionel unexpectedly arrives in Smallville and tells the LutherCorp Plant employees that the plant is being shut down. Lex refuses to return to Metropolis, and plans an employee buyout. Lionel buys the Smallville bank so he can foreclose on the employees if they default. Roger Nixon steals the octagonal disk from Lex's desk, then booby-traps the Kents' truck, filming Clark as he miraculously survives. Nixon then tells Clark he wants to write a story about him. The reporter also discovers the spaceship in the Kents' storm cellar. The octagonal disk spins from Nixon's grasp and fits into a slot in the ship. As the weather deteriorates, the ship powers up.

Whitney decides to join the Marines, leaving Smallville on the night of the Spring Formal. He asks Clark to look after Lana, and she then drives Whitney to the bus station.

With twisters threatening Smallville, Lionel and Lex have a showdown in the mansion, which is interrupted when a tornado hits, leaving Lionel crushed beneath a pillar. The Kents discover Nixon in the cellar, and Jonathan chases the reporter out into the storm to retrieve the videotape of Clark. Driving back from the bus station, Lana is caught in the tornado. Clark abandons Chloe at the dance to check on Lana and arrives just as her truck is caught up in the twister... ■

Smallville ⬤ Ledger

* * * Volume 64, Number 13 * * *

LUTHORCORP PLANT TO CLOSE
Lionel Luthor Destroys Smallville's Economy In One Minute; Blames Son

In a shocking surprise announcement, LuthorCorp CEO Lionel Luthor has permanently shut down LuthorCorp's Smallville base of operations, Fertilizer Plant No.#3, blaming plant president Lex Luthor for mismanagement and leaving approximately 2,500 employees out of work.

Stunned silence and tears followed the speech as workers milled about, wondering whether or not to return to their workstations. While most people hugged and consoled one another, some were overheard cursing Lex, who instantly fled the premises.

By Christopher James Beppo

Opposite: Clark races to rescue Lana.

TEMPEST: IN DEPTH

"It's fun watching all the little bits and pieces behind the scenes and seeing how it all fits together. There are things you wouldn't think about watching it." — Gregory Slay, Remy Zero

"Tempest' was insanity at its finest," Mike Walls says, smiling hugely. "There couldn't be enough wind for Greg [Beeman], and he couldn't make his shots wide enough. We brought up jet-powered wind machines from the States that they'd used for the movie *Twister!*" "We are going to be performing two of our songs, there's beautiful women, a great plotline, possible mass destruction and all kinds of drama!" As Gregory Slay of Remy Zero said in his promo for 'Tempest', the season finale was unmissable.

"It was a great script, and we all knew that right away," Greg Beeman says. "It's always good in television when you get a great script to direct. Sometimes you get an okay script, and you work hard to make it better. There's a countdown on every show — you get the script and have six or seven days before you start shooting it. Not only do you have to figure out how you're going to shoot it and organize it, but if it's not so good, you have to make it better. 'Tempest' was good right away."

Although writers Gough and Millar were very taken with Jeph Loeb's graphic novel *Superman For All Seasons*, the tornadoes that hit Smallville in Loeb's story weren't the inspiration for the storms in 'Tempest'. "We had always wanted to do the twisters," Millar explains. "We always imagined that the end of the season would be the prom and the twisters. The idea came from a true story we heard on the radio about a high school that was hit by tornadoes on prom night."

As director, Greg Beeman set a visual tone for the episode from the very first scene. "I immediately had the idea of using the rising storm thematically," he explains, "so everything started calmly and started to build. I began with Lex being blasted by the wind from the helicopter landing as Lionel arrives to shut the plant down. I wanted to set the mood for the storm which was coming. Then everything settles down, and the show starts calmly, but then as it builds the camera starts to move more and circle more, until the storm arrives and it builds to this fever pitch. The whole episode had this steady, graceful arc to chaos, which I really tried to control."

"The whole episode really builds," Miles Millar agrees. "Everything is being set up, and at the end you have the payoff with Lex and Lionel, and then the tornadoes coming in, which is just really cool. Greg did a fantastic job directing it, and made it a really good send-off."

"Controlling it was hard," Beeman admits. "I had to try to control the build so that as the drama built, the visual style built and the wind built. The wind gets introduced in a very gentle way when Chloe picks up Clark in front of his house, and from then on, in every single scene we took great care to add a little bit more and then a little bit more. When Lana drops Whitney off at the bus station there is a lot of wind, and then the

Opposite: Clark with the spaceship that brought him to Earth.

Above: The cast join Remy Zero on stage during the filming of 'Tempest'.

Opposite: A romantic dance for Clark and Chloe.

episode builds to this huge action packed finale with Lex fighting his father and the spaceship coming to life with Roger Nixon."

Beeman thinks that 'Tempest' is a good example of his dictum that "*Smallville* is seen and experienced from the point of view of a teenager. That means that everything is strongly felt. If you're in love, you're head over heels in love. If you're scared, you're terrified. If you're sad, you're in grief. The emotions are strong, but it doesn't mean that the performances are over-the-top. It means that whatever is happening matters — to the person and to the filmmaker. In 'Tempest', the emotions are very strong. Whitney is leaving; Lana is in distress and she's weeping as she's driving home; Clark and Chloe are nervously experimenting whether they'll be in love; Roger Nixon is evil; Jonathan Kent is fighting to protect his family; and Lex and his father are battling. In some ways it's operatic, but to direct operatic performances and not have it go over the top is tricky. It's actually more subtle than it sounds. You have to feel it more than show it. If the director is passionate and experiences his part of the process passionately, then it shows up on film. I think my main job is to make people believe in the material. However you experience and communicate your passion will transfer to other people."

The crew enjoyed working with Beeman on the episode, although it stretched

Above: Martha tries to stop Jonathan from attacking Roger Nixon.

everyone to their limits. "I don't think as a crew we ever worked harder than we did on that episode," Mike Walsh recalls. "We were going all-out as fast as we could go to try to get it all done. The sequence with Lana in the truck had such scope — it was amazing that Greg was able to get what he got. To this day I can't say how we pulled it off, because I was just running like crazy for nine days trying to get it all to happen."

"That season finale was a big show," construction coordinator and production designer for this episode, Rob Maier, remembers. "Greg was phenomenal. He had a tremendous amount of energy. You give him a set and he'll shoot every last inch of it. We did a ton of stuff out at the Kent Farm location, and filmed out at Zero Avenue (the road running along the US/Canada border) for the scene where the tornadoes start to skip along. We blew out the window on the Luthor mansion. We wrecked the storm cellar."

The cast were equally excited about the episode, with Tom Welling commenting that "the season finale was huge", while Kristin Kreuk was bubbling over with enthusiasm about the "incredible" story. "There are so many things going on," she points out. "There are tornadoes and spaceships, romances blossoming, people on the verge of leaving, plants closing down, and people's lives changing."

Kristin was also pleased with the emotional developments in the episode. "I think Lana definitely feels a little jealous during this, and she doesn't want to be," she says. "Clark has known Chloe for a long time, and he's slowly beginning to see her in a new light. Lana is trying to support him in that, and it's really hard. I like the way that *Smallville* has people having to deal with their feelings on their own, and having to overcome obstacles, just like in real life."

Allison Mack particularly relished the "nice little scenes between Tom and me. I liked the moment when I picked him up at the farm. That was difficult, though, because I was wearing that beautiful dress that they had made for me, and Jimmy Choo shoes with really high heels. We're out at the farm, with all the rocks and gravel — and I had to run across to him in these little shoes. I was lucky I didn't break an ankle!"

The actress laughs when she recalls a slight practical problem with her dress. "It was strapless," she points out, "and it had a big train on it. Tom had to run behind me, and he kept stepping on the train, which meant my dress was being pulled lower and lower!"

Eric Johnson enjoyed his final opportunity to show Whitney's tender side. "He and Lana have their little private dance before the Spring Formal," he says, "and it's really sweet and romantic. That's a side of Whitney I was always trying to tell people about —

Below: Lana and Whitney share a final dance.

he's a nice guy and he likes Lana a lot. The season finale showed a little more of his emotional side."

The scene in which Whitney asks Clark to look after Lana was the last scene to be filmed by Eric Johnson as a regular actor on the program. "I channeled my own feelings through in that," Eric recalls. "We did my close up last. It was really emotional for me. I wasn't crying, but it felt odd because my character was going off to war, and I was really leaving the show."

"Whitney going off to war was something that we came up with in the middle of the season," Miles Millar recalls. "We didn't want to kill him, because we potentially wanted him to come back, but we really liked the idea of a noble, heroic send-off."

The cast enjoyed the opportunity to hang out with the band whose song had embodied the show for them in the opening titles. "It's such a great song," Tom Welling says. "It gets you going — the song gets the excitement level up to start the show." Al Gough adds, "Lyrically it obviously works. We wanted something that had a male vibe — the other WB shows had themes sung by females. We looked at songs by different artists, but with 'Save Me', the feel was good, the lyrics were good, and when we put it up against the cut title sequence it played really well."

Below: Filming Lana's truck accident.

Remy Zero were also delighted to be part of the *Smallville* experience. "We all grew

Above: Lana crawls from the truck...

up in loads of Smallvilles," Gregory Slay points out. "We couldn't believe it when we were asked to appear in the episode."

For the band, it was an introduction to the unusual way in which scenes of live music are filmed for television. Although the end result makes it seem that Remy Zero were playing away at full volume throughout the scenes at the Spring Formal, it would be impossible for everything to be filmed and recorded if that had been the case. "People had to dance without making noise," Remy Zero's Cinjun Tate recalls, "and sometimes we had to play without making noise, because there was dialog that had to be recorded. Then there are other times where we had to be loud. It's crazy, but a lot of fun to do."

Michael Rosenbaum found the climactic scenes at the Luthor mansion challenging to film. He believes that Lex really considered letting his father die after the beam crashes down on him. "At that point in his life, he has almost given up on his father," he notes. "It was one of those times when he was very close to becoming the Lex that we know he will eventually become. If he had let his father die, it would have been his 'turn to the dark side', and just for a moment, I think he was thinking, 'Screw you, you son of a bitch.' He forgot who he was."

The actor admits that "I had trouble in that scene. Sometimes as an actor, you're missing something. I will not let something go if I don't believe what I'm doing. If it doesn't feel believable then I want to do another take. That scene in 'Tempest' was the only time that I wanted to do another take for that reason. I didn't feel as if it was working. I asked John [Glover] what I was doing wrong, and he told me that 'the most simple thing I learned as an actor in Acting 101 was to listen and be specific.' After he said that, I said, 'Say no more,' and the next take was magic, because I just listened. As actors, we forget all the time to listen. It's a basic rule — if you just listen, you're fine. Afterward I thanked him and gave him a big hug."

To film the scene, the construction crew knew which beam would be coming down, but didn't know until the day of the shoot how Beeman intended to shoot it. "We were flying by the seat of the pants, and it worked out," Mike Walsh recalls. "It all happened in the right order, because we were working to the master plan that Greg had worked out, which was perfect."

"We had a stunt double for the actual hit, because we had the debris flying around," stunt coordinator Lauro Chartrand adds. "Then we put the beam on John, and had him fall down with it. He didn't take the initial force!"

The wind effects are some of the strongest memories that the cast carry with them from that episode. Even the smallest piece of debris being blown around a set at the wind speeds that were being created becomes potentially dangerous. "When you have high speed fans going full blast and you're shooting debris through the shot, sometimes, just

sometimes, a piece of that high speed foliage might hit you square in the noggin," Eric Johnson comments wryly.

Annette O'Toole has a similar memory of her final scene, "where Jonathan leaves me in the cellar. He's going out into the storm and I'm worried about him and I scream, 'Jonathan!' I looked up and there was a special effects guy throwing leaves down at me, because the hurricane was happening outside the cellar. They had a fan going and the leaves flying around and this guy throwing these things. The leaves hit me in the mouth and I was inhaling them. Greg Beeman quickly called cut, and said, 'Hey, man, don't throw the leaves directly in her face!' They don't know until they start doing it where it's going to hit you and where it's going to go. Who would think you'd be cut by a leaf? But they're dry, and they have stems and stuff on them!"

John Schneider enjoyed the scene because "that was the first time the spaceship gave us information, the first time it glowed. It was our first indication of where Clark came from. When that spaceship lit up, it was the first kind of sci-fi aspect of the legend. I think that's where *Smallville* really started to build up a dual head of steam — we're very normal, yet we're very sci-fi at the same time."

"That episode was so intense," Eric Johnson comments. "It was one of the biggest hours of television I've ever watched." The episode ends on a cliffhanger that surprised everyone on both sides of the screen. "We couldn't believe that they stopped there," Mike Walls says. "We were ready to shoot the next part of it! 'Tempest' was an amazing emotional ride that everybody in the cast and crew went on." ■

CLARK KENT

"I'm hanging out in a graveyard. Does this strike you as okay behavior?"

"Clark doesn't always have a handle on life," says Tom Welling. "He's still a kid who's trying to figure out what's going on. Our show is about him trying to control his powers and work things out for the best, for everyone." As Tom Welling regularly points out, he's not playing Superman — he's playing Clark Kent, who, unknown to him at the time *Smallville* is set, is going to grow up to become the defender of truth, justice, and the American way. But for now, all Clark Kent wants is to be an average guy and fit in with his peers at school. "I always saw there was more to it than Superman," Tom says. "*Smallville* isn't about Clark Kent being a super hero, it's about Clark Kent trying to be a normal teenager. When I read the pilot script, it was even more interesting than I thought it was going to be. I had thought it was just going to be — as it's still wrongly described by some people now — 'Superman in High School', but it definitely has a different spin. It was uncharted territory that focused more on Clark, and how these abilities helped other people, but didn't necessarily help him. They made it more difficult for him, and alienated him from others. It's a classic coming of age story. Clark is always trying to get a hold of what's going on internally and externally."

Tom himself was a reluctant super hero. The former construction worker became a model when he was spotted on holiday in Nantucket with a couple of friends. He went on to become the face of Abercrombie & Fitch, and traveled the world on modeling shoots before making the leap into acting. He appeared in commercials for the phone company Verizon and then played opposite Amy Brennerman for six episodes in the series *Judging Amy*. That led to the role of Clark Kent. "Apparently I came in late in the audition process," he explains. "They said they'd been looking for Clark Kent for six months. Then I came in, and everything moved pretty quickly after that. There were two or three auditions — for the casting director, and then the network and the studio — and then here we were in Vancouver shooting the pilot."

Tom freely concedes that he wasn't a massive Superman fan when he took the role, but points out that even if he had been, watching the big screen *Superman* films from the late Seventies and Eighties starring Christopher Reeve wouldn't necessarily have helped him. "I don't have a lot of knowledge of what happened in those films," he says. "I remember watching them growing up, but I didn't follow the mythology all that much. When I came onto *Smallville*, I didn't have that knowledge floating around in my head. I haven't gone in there researching Superman or Clark Kent, because I don't think that would help me at all. I think it's important to take this material that Al Gough and Miles Millar have set up for us. I play Clark with the information that *Smallville* gives me within the script. When I got this job, a lot of people gave me a lot of gifts — books and toys about Superman — and they're all sitting on a shelf. Maybe someday when the show's over I'll take a look at them, but right

now I'm just looking at the script that I'm given."

Tom sees the relationship between Clark and Lana as central to the show. "By the end of the first episode, he's made a connection with her on a lot of levels," he says. "He finds Lana in the graveyard at a time when he doesn't know which way is up. He discovers she is someone he can really talk to. It's the first time in his life he's found someone who really understands him. It brings them close — not as close as Clark would like, but at the end of that episode, he imagines that he's with her and can really see it happening."

Not having someone that he can share his secrets with was definitely a problem for Clark during the first year. "He is burdened with a lot of responsibility," Tom notes. "He hasn't been able to choose whether or not he has these abilities. All this responsibility has just been thrust on him, and he has to deal with it. There have got to be times when he goes home and thinks to himself, 'Why me?' He wishes it could all go away and he could just be normal. That's part of the character dilemma which makes him interesting to play."

Even though there's a connection with Lana, Clark knows that he can't be fully honest with her, and that causes a rift between them. "He can't open up and expose himself to Lana because he fears that she won't understand who he is, and won't accept him for who he is," Tom says. "He arrived in the meteor shower that killed her parents, and his fear that she will totally kick him out of her life is enough to persuade him to keep his mouth shut."

The secret of Clark's superhuman abilities also prevents him from having the relationship with Lex Luthor that Clark would ideally like. It may be an unusual pairing between the farmboy and the city sophisticate, but "Clark and Lex both want a real friendship," Tom maintains. "However, Lex can't tell Clark everything, and Clark can't tell him everything. There's always a line between them."

Tom maintains that the key to Clark is to remember that he is still a high school kid. "Going into that first audition, I didn't know how anyone could prepare to play this role," he recalls, "and as I was waiting in the room to go in to the audition, I realized that you just have to take everything that makes this kid a super hero, and throw it out the window. I had to do it just like a normal kid — the special effects and everything else would help fill in the blanks — and that's how I try to attack this material.

"I love going to work," Tom says in conclusion, adding with a laugh, "I love coming home from work, and I love the bit in between!" ▪

LANA LANG

"Maybe I should just accept my destiny. All I'm ever going to be is a little girl in a fairy princess costume who lost her parents."

"I had no clue who Lana Lang was when I was cast," Kristin Kreuk laughs. "My uncle had a comic book store when I was growing up, so he knew who she was, and I learned a little bit about her from the producers. Now I've learned a lot about the history and the mythology and I think she's really a different person in the show than how she's been portrayed in the comic books. I'm learning about Lana as we go along."

The Canadian actress was best known for playing the title character in Hallmark's version of *Snow White* before she landed the part of Lana Lang in *Smallville*. Shortly before she got the role she had decided to get an agent, and went to the audition for the show in Los Angeles after the producers had seen a tape of her performance. "I had only then decided that I was going to try acting," she explains, "and originally I was just going on auditions in Vancouver.

"In the pilot, Lana was presented as this beautiful, popular girl who is really lonely," Kristin continues. "She has this big hole in her heart because her parents died when she was young. But she is also very strong and intelligent. She's very empathetic to everybody, especially to Clark because she felt a connection to him, particularly in the graveyard scene. I think she just saw him as this kindred spirit that's just so sad and lonely. She's the girl he's watched the whole time — but it's completely innocent. He's sweet and completely endearing, and I think she could see that from the beginning — it was pretty damn obvious!"

When the series began, and throughout the first season, Lana was more or less involved with high school jock Whitney Fordman. "I think one of the downfalls of that relationship and the way it was portrayed was that you never really got to know Whitney," Kristin maintains. "You only saw what Clark saw of him, and I think Lana is smarter than that. She wasn't with him just because her aunt wanted her to be with him. And she wasn't with him just because he was the star quarterback. She was with him because she really did love him. But I don't think Lana was still in love with Whitney when we started in the pilot. I think she was at one time, but she'd come to a point where she was just comfortable with him. She'd known him a long time, so they had a good friendship."

Kristin believes part of the reason that Lana was a bit retiring in the first season was because "she was never really put in situations where she had the opportunity to be outgoing. She communicated purely with Whitney and Clark. And that was it. There was a random scene with Lex every once in a while, but you never saw her in any social situations. At her birthday party, she goes outside and doesn't want to deal with it! I think she lived in her head a little bit. Lana's the type of girl that would read romantic novels on the sly, even though she's smart and she'd also read the classics."

LANA LANG

The actress believes that Lana's character evolution seriously began in 'X-Ray', when she realized that the image that she had of her parents might not necessarily be the case. When she hears her mother's cutting graduation speech, she realizes that her mother wasn't who she had believed. "She has this fantasy in her head of what her mom was like, and she wants to be like that," she explains. "Lana grew up with her aunt Nell, who I've always pictured as somebody who was very materialistic. She was very concerned about appearances. She'd tell Lana that she had to look this way, and do things a certain way so that people thought good things about her. So Lana grew up thinking that this was what she had to do, and what she had to be."

Kristin feels that Lana is intrinsically "a tough girl. Lex really brings that out in her — he brings out her dark side. He's very much like his father. As she discovers herself more, and feels more comfortable with who she is, she's willing to do things that before she would have thought were not right. I was all for her investigating the other coffee shop in 'Drone'. She had every right to do that. She was being a business person!"

Kristin always felt that like her classmates, Lana harbored dreams of getting away from Smallville, and in the first season there were little hints of what might come in her future. "Everyone else has these plans for their future, but she's stuck in Smallville, and stuck in her past. I thought in the beginning that that was a part of her, but that she also had ambitions and dreams to go to Metropolis and be somebody, and that somehow she was going to find a way to do it. That was even reflected in her bedroom. In season one, she had posters of all the movie stars and posters of the buildings in Metropolis, and then she had her horses and the different kinds of books and the pictures of her childhood. There was an amalgamation of stuff of who she was."

Kristin enjoyed the opportunities presented in the first season for Lana to be a little different. "The scene in 'X-Ray' where I played Tina Greer with Whitney in the hallway was so much fun to do," she recalls. "That was so not what Lana is normally like — she was sexy and manipulative — and when the producers saw that, they decided to write 'Nicodemus' for me."

'Nicodemus' allowed Kristin to stretch some acting muscles that weren't normally used for Lana during the first year. "I was thrilled by that episode, because it gave me an opportunity to do something new," she admits. However, although she was happy to participate in the stuntwork involved in the episode, she very firmly made it clear to the producers that she was not prepared to wear the sexy

lingerie that the scene in the swimming pool called for. "I just didn't think it was appropriate, and I didn't think red lace underwear was really appropriate for a fifteen-year-old girl."

The actress thinks that "Lana needs to be on her own. I think she's got to learn not to lean on a guy. She hasn't really been in that situation — she's had that opportunity a bit, but there's always somebody there. I think she needs to be needed. She's never had anyone in her life that's completely consistent. I can see her getting darker, because she has that in her.

"I'm excited to see what the writers' vision of her ends up being, because it's probably a little different from mine. That's the interesting thing, because it keeps me on my toes. I still care about Lana, but I've realized that what happens to her is really out of my hands! They have whatever fun they're going to have, and I'm just going to leave it to them, and trust them to take her in the right direction." ■

LEX LUTHOR

"I've always been fighting my destiny, trying to avoid becoming my father. But we all have certain genes that, no matter how much we want to change, dominate us."

"What are 700 other actors not doing that I need to do?" Michael Rosenbaum recalls thinking when he was preparing to audition for Lex Luthor. Although he had already been in for one audition for the part, Michael admits that he hadn't taken it that seriously at the time. When a second chance arose, he did his homework, going through the two-and-a-half-page scene between Lex and Clark in the mansion from the pilot, and indicating all the places where he would be funny, charismatic or menacing as appropriate. "I went in and I just took over," he explains. "I was really confident, because I had nothing to lose."

Michael's confidence impressed the producers so much that they offered him the job. The actor was at the time better known for his comedy roles on *The Tom Show*, and *Zoe, Duncan, Jack & Jane*, and was delighted to have an opportunity to demonstrate his dramatic talents. "I always said I was going to show my stuff one day," he recalls, "and once I'd shaved my head, everyone looked at me in a different light. People now think of me as a serious actor. I always knew I could do it. With this part, and the writing, and what Al and Miles and the rest of the *Smallville* crew brought to it, the way people perceived me has been different. It just changed my life and I'm grateful for that."

He was equally pleased that the producers didn't want the Lex Luthor of *Smallville* to be a precursor to the comedy villain Gene Hackman portrayed in the movies. "They wanted a real quality about him," Michael explains, "a genuine likeability and a vulnerability. I want people to like him — he's not some goofy character. I think that he is really trying to be a hero. There's an ambiguous feeling you get when you watch him." Rosenbaum enjoys the "little tastes when you think Lex has gone bad, and this is the end, but then you realize that he is fighting with all his might *not* to go that way. It's hard for him. I think the reason why people are embracing the character is that they can see themselves in that position."

Michael doesn't think that Lex always has shady ulterior motives; a lot of what he does is driven by simple curiosity. After all, not long after he arrives in Smallville, he's involved in a very bizarre accident. "Look at the situation at the start of the series," the actor points out. "If you crash into someone at sixty-five miles an hour, and the last thing you remember is hitting him before you go off the bridge, and you're alive and he's unscathed — there's something majorly wrong! Then there are all these curious things that are happening around Smallville. Why is Clark Kent always involved with them? Who wouldn't want to delve into that, especially when there's nothing else really to do in Smallville? For Lex, it's either take a nice ride to Metropolis and work with his dad, or find out what's going on with this strong, strange fellow, Clark Kent."

But there's more than that to the young Luthor. Michael feels that Lex is always searching for unconditional love. "That's all he wants," he claims. "I think we all do. And what's so sad about Lex, he can't find it in any of the women that he tries to invest himself in. He can't find it with his father. The only person who might have loved him is his mother who died so young, or his brother who died. Everybody he touches ends up either crossing him or trying to kill him. I think Lex is trying to be a hero." Both Michael and Annette O'Toole recognize the yearning that Lex has for a mother figure in his life, "and we play it that Lex and Martha do have this connection," Michael says. "She wants to be the mother that he lost, and he wants her to be that. I always like to look at her in a certain way."

The actor believes that Lex is involved with Lana partly because he feels a connection to her as a result of the traumatic events of October 16, 1989. "His life changed the same day hers did," he notes. "They don't really discuss that ever, but he looks at her and says to himself, 'Hey, that day you lost a part of you, and that day I lost a big part of me.' I think they see that in each other. I also think Lex really cares for Clark and wants to see him get the girl. Ultimately, I think Lex wants to see Lana grow into the woman that she has the potential to be. He wants to see her trusting herself and getting to be who she wants to be."

Michael has liked the chances to show the depths of Lex's anger. "It's fun when you get the chance to go overboard," he says. "When they give you something like 'Hug' where you come out with the machine gun and shoot it — you're the bad guy for a second. It gives the fans that little taste of who Lex will be. It's building up inside him."

He also thinks that the end of the first season gave a great insight into Lex's psyche and the tempestuous relationship between Lex and his father. "I think the thing that separates a murderer from a regular person who's sane is that one moment of decision," he explains. "Murderers can make the decision to commit

that act and kill, which most people probably never have to face. You or I have never been pushed that far, and in comparison to Lex's life, our lives haven't been that traumatic. For that moment in the library, Lex forgot who he was. That's the way I played it, and that's the way I wanted it to come across. And it's those decisions that you make that make you realize that there's such a fine line between rational and irrational. When you're driving down the road, your day's just gone to hell, and you're really upset, for a moment you just want to jerk the wheel off the road. Most people just think that for a second then let it go, but at the moment when you think it, are you really contemplating it? Would you really do that? Most people wouldn't, but when he sees his father lying there, it's one of those moments where Lex is like that driver."

Although Michael doesn't know all the details about the journey along the way, he does know what ultimately turns Lex away from his friendship with Clark. "I'm sworn to secrecy," he says firmly. "I can tell you, though, that throughout the show thus far, the whole thing about friendship that Lex says to Clark is pretty much etched in stone, that's how important it is to him." ▪

PETE ROSS

"No offense, Clark, but digging up six pages of interesting on you is going to require some serious excavation..."

"Pete has no powers," Sam Jones III points out. "Clark has the powers. Pete's not psychic. He's just a friend. To me, he's a hero in his own way by being a good friend to Clark, and just being a good listener. I think the big moments are when Clark and Pete share a smile."

Sam was delighted when he was cast as Pete Ross a mere four days before filming began on *Smallville*'s pilot. The young actor had come out to Hollywood and had a successful run as a guest star on numerous series, including *NYPD Blue* and *CSI: Crime Scene Investigation*, as well as playing the title character in the movie *ZigZag*, giving him the opportunity to work with such talented actors as Wesley Snipes, John Leguizamo and Oliver Platt. "I've been pretty lucky and blessed in my career," Sam comments. "Everything's always been right there for me. I came out with no real acting experience, and I heard a lot of bad things about Hollywood, but luckily none of it came to be true in my situation."

He was just completing filming on *ZigZag* when his agent told him about the potential opportunity on a new show. "When my agent called me and told me about this show called *Smallville*, I wasn't so sure, because she said it was about Superman," Sam recalls. "I thought it was going to be cheesy, but then she sent me over the sides and the script, and the script seemed pretty good." Sam was impressed from the get-go since very unusually, his audition was held at one of the producers' houses on a Sunday afternoon. Within a few days he had been cast, and was heading to Vancouver to shoot the pilot. "They just hadn't found the right person for Pete," Sam says, "and I guess I was the right person."

In the DC Comics mythology, Pete Ross is Caucasian, and Sam was very pleased that the producers cast an African-American in the role. "I knew when the opportunity came that me being on *Smallville* was definitely going to be a blessing, because everything to do with Superman usually goes down in history," he says. "When I found out that Pete Ross is a white guy, it was even more of an honor that the WB would take that risk. I would have understood if they had created a new black character for *Smallville*, but they actually went and changed the ethnicity of this character from the comics. They just cast it colorblind. Every race came in, and they looked high and low. I think they were looking for months."

Like a number of his colleagues in the cast, Sam wasn't a great Superman fan when he started working on the series. "When I was younger, I was into Superman, but I wasn't into comic books," he explains. "I had a lot of comic books because one of my uncles had a lot of them and he gave them to us and we looked through them. We knew who Superman was, and one Halloween I dressed up like Superman. I had the pajamas

and when they got too big, my mom cut the feet off at the bottom. I used to run around the house with a towel around my neck as a cape. But I wouldn't say that I knew the mythology."

Sam admits that he was also a relative newcomer to television production when he joined the cast of *Smallville*, since this was his first job as a series regular. "I was simply amazed by the quality of the pilot," he recalls. "I don't think I knew director David Nutter's caliber at the time, or what the show was going to be like, I was just doing my acting. The next thing I know, we had a screening of the pilot in a movie theater, and I was blown away with the effects, the color, and the crispness of the show. It was just great to be part of something so spectacular."

Initially Sam was told that Clark, Pete and Chloe "get along because basically we're outcasts. We're not really good at sports, and we're a quirky trio. As the season progressed, we became more like regular kids who just get along." Pete's role in the series often became as a sounding board for Clark, even though he can't tell him his biggest secret. Sam admits that during that first season, he initially thought that "Pete should be getting more air time. He should be doing this, or that. But I grew to realize that *Smallville* is more about Clark's journey every day. In the first season, we were getting to meet the characters and understand where they're coming from, but it's mostly about Clark's journey. The rest of us are there to help out the story as best we can every week."

Not surprisingly, Sam enjoyed the first season episodes where the spotlight was on Pete. He relished being pursued by the Freak of the Week in 'Craving', and reserves special praise for 'Nicodemus', in which he got to play a powerful scene with Michael Rosenbaum when Pete discovers Lex discussing a cure for the Nicodemus flower with Dr. Hamilton and threatens his life. "Michael's a great actor, and it's really fun working with him," he says. "I had an awesome time on that episode, just being able to switch it up. Pete's usually so innocent and happy-go-lucky, so being able to get a little bit of a dark side was really fun! I got to play both sides of the spectrum in that episode."

Sam wasn't surprised that the potential interest Pete showed in Chloe in the pilot wasn't followed up during the first year. "Their relationship is tricky," he admits. "In the beginning, Pete definitely had a crush on Chloe, but that's been complicated by the whole Clark/Lana/Chloe deal. That also shows how Pete is such a good friend. I think he observes, and keeps his feelings to himself. Sometimes you're friends with people but you have a crush on them, but as you become better friends, the crush stops. They have an extremely valuable friendship. The more they've hung out together, the stronger their friendship is. They understand each other and I think they click and work well together."

From early on, the actor has had plans of how he would like to see Pete grow and mature. "He has been mature, but I want to get him to a point where he still has his happy-go-lucky-ness, but at the same time has a degree of depth."

Sam doesn't disguise the fact that he's a great fan of the show. "We film the episodes, sure, but then actually watching them is so different," he explains. "In my head, I imagine them perfectly — but then they take them to a whole other level. I'm just glad to be a part of a production like this! It feels really good to be a part of something so positive. To see that the people at home are watching and liking what I'm doing really makes me happy." ▪

CHLOE SULLIVAN

"I have this horrible nightmare that you are going to rush to the bus station after Whitney leaves and profess your undying love for Lana, and I'm going to be waiting at the gym all alone, and if you do that to me Clark, I will never speak to you again..."

"I look for something that's different," Allison Mack admits. "I look for scripts which are well-written with interesting dialog and interesting characters." An actress since the age of four, Allison started out appearing in a German chocolate commercial before graduating to roles in *Police Academy 6: City Under Siege* and the third *Honey, I Shrunk the Kids* film, *Honey, We Shrunk Ourselves*, an experience which introduced her to the specific requirements of acting alongside special effects that aren't seen by the actors in the studio. "That was all greenscreen," she recalls, "so I'm pretty used to working with effects."

Smallville's casting director, Dee Dee Bradley, had actually cast Allison in her very first TV series when she was only seven years old, and when Dee Dee told her about the show, Allison initially considered the part of Lana before auditioning twice for the role of Chloe. "Because of Dee Dee I went back in," Allison points out. "She rang me when I was just going on vacation and said I had to come in for the second audition. I went into it with a very flippant attitude, and of course that worked perfectly for Chloe."

Allison had been a little surprised to find herself the only Caucasian actress up for the role when she first auditioned. "I wondered if I was at the wrong audition," she says. "There were all these African-American women sitting in a room — and me." The original plans for the character had called for an ethnic background, and the producers experimented with various different combinations of ethnicity before they decided on the mix that finally made it to the screen. When Allison reauditioned, the producers realized that she had exactly what they were looking for, and Allison recalls the pilot's director, David Nutter, "winking at me and shaking my hand after the audition. I was wondering what the heck he was trying to tell me, and a couple of hours later I found out that I'd booked the job."

In the early days, Allison considers that Chloe was "one of the misfits. She doesn't fit in at high school. It was pretty obvious that she was just a really smart girl with attitude. I knew she liked Clark, because they wrote that in the pilot, but they never really wrote how much she liked him. Al and Miles developed it into this really huge storyline that allowed my character to progress."

Allison likes the fact that, in common with Lionel Luthor, Chloe Sullivan was created specifically for *Smallville* by Al Gough and Miles Millar. "I really feel like she's mine, and I don't have to worry about copying anyone else's performance," she says. "It's been a real team effort between me and the writers. We've gotten to develop the

character together. I love how intelligently she's written, and yet I still have to find ways to have fun with it — and it has been fun."

The actress doesn't subscribe to the fan theory that at some point down the line Chloe is going to change her name, and she's really Lois Lane, Clark/Superman's future bride. "Clark doesn't love her, and I don't think that would change," she says firmly, "so she could never be Lois. It's a good theory, and it'll be interesting to see what happens if Lois is introduced on the show."

Allison is very happy that Chloe hasn't had her own long-term love interest on the show as yet. "I like the fact that she's independent, and doing her own thing without anyone," she says. "It's important to portray a woman like that. Lana is so involved with the love story with Clark that she fulfils that. We definitely need a woman on the show who is independent and doesn't have a person that she uses as a crutch."

She sees Chloe as "a 'big city' girl stuck in a farm town. She's been there for five or six years. In 'Obscura' there's the really sweet scene between Clark and Lana where he remembers that the second that Chloe got to Smallville, she asked where she could get a newspaper. This is something this girl's always been obsessed with. I think her brain works faster than the average person's. She's always curious and wanting to know the truth. She wants to be honest with people. She wants to understand things and expose falsehoods. I think that's what drives her."

Although Allison doesn't think that Chloe should have a boyfriend to use as an emotional crutch, she notes that "her whole ambition and falling into journalism is a nice escape for her. It's something good for her to focus on so she doesn't have to focus on other things. Any time that Chloe is upset, she never just sits there and allows herself to be upset — she is always doing something."

Like her castmates, Allison enjoys the atmosphere on the *Smallville* set. "I like to have fun," she laughs. "I'm just a big goofball and I like to have a good time. The best part of my job is being able to play make believe for a living. As an actor, you never have to grow up. That's one of the greatest gifts of my job. I don't have to become an adult. I can just pretend I'm someone else all the time." ∎

WHITNEY FORDMAN

"I don't want to be a 'remember him?' — Smallville's got enough of those guys."

"Playing Whitney was the greatest job in the world," Eric Johnson says firmly. "My friends would call me and tell me I was a lucky guy. I went to work, played football, and got to pretend that Kristin Kreuk was my girlfriend. I made a lot of good friends on the show as well."

A native of Edmonton, Alberta, Eric moved to Vancouver to work on *Smallville* after he was cast as Lana's boyfriend. He originally auditioned for the part of Lex Luthor in December 2000, and then continued auditioning for other characters, including Clark Kent. "The producers wanted me to come down to Los Angeles to audition, but I said that they had seen what I could do with a bigger character, and if they wanted me down there, they must bring me down to screen test," Eric recalls. "It was a gamble, but they brought me down, screen-tested me, and I got the part. It was the easiest pilot season I ever had — I was in Los Angeles for all of a day!"

Eric couldn't remotely be described as a Superman fan before he started work on the show. "I'd never read Superman comics, and I'd not seen the movies," he admits. Researching Superman on the Internet, he was amazed to discover that there was already a fansite dedicated to the show, even before the pilot had been filmed. "When I saw that, I realized *Smallville* was going to be huge. What's there not to love about the show? It's great entertainment. It's got a little bit of comedy, action, special effects, and the legend of Superman. You can't beat that."

Going into the first season, neither the producers nor Eric wanted Whitney to be "the stereotypical jock", the actor recalls. "There has to be more to him than just football and girls, or it makes Lana look stupid."

Eric thinks it was unfortunate that a lot of the audience "took that scarecrow thing in the pilot very seriously. There were allusions to some really dark stuff there. It's very hard to change people's minds once they have an opinion — and you don't have time necessarily in the forty-five minutes of an episode to do much. But they did more with my character in that first season than anyone else's. I think I had more storylines going on than anybody else. Most people didn't see that, but they tried very hard to get my character on the other side in people's minds."

For Eric, 'Kinetic' marked a turning point in the year. "It was the first episode where I went in to work every day," he recalls, "and I had so much fun. The rest of the year, I was just so happy to be there. I wasn't nervous or tense. There was an evolution in the character that was invigorating."

Eric admits that when he read the pilot script, he realized that "this character had a limited life. I didn't know how long he would be around for, but I knew it wasn't going to be for the full run of the show. When we started the series, and they were moving my

story along pretty quickly, I had a feeling they wouldn't be able to keep this up. There were times when I'd get the script, and it would be frustrating because I wasn't in it, but I totally knew that that was going to be happening. They were very up front about that."

The producers were also very open with Eric about Whitney's departure at the end of the first season. "They told me that I wasn't going to be coming back in the same capacity in the second year in 'Obscura', when I found my father's war medals," he remembers. "It was in the script, so they had to let me know. Greg Beeman took me out for a drink, and everything was going through my mind. Were they going to kill me off? Had I done something wrong? When he told me that Whitney was joining up, I didn't feel as bad about it as I thought I was going to. I had had a lot of fun, and I would come back the following year and have a swan song."

Eric enjoyed the physical aspects of playing Whitney, particularly out on the football field. "I tried to do as much as I possibly could. I wanted to do absolutely everything, but they couldn't let me. When we were filming 'Hothead', I had to throw the ball right up into camera," he remembers, "and then I got hit right away. I started bugging the guy who was hitting me. He used to play for the BC Lions, the local team in Vancouver, and I was asking if that was as hard as he could hit. Was that all he had? 'I played high school football,' I said to him, 'and we had girls on our team who hit harder than you.' He just kept hitting me harder and harder — and I was having such a great time."

The actor laughs about one aspect of Whitney that fans picked up on very early — his unfortunate record with motorized vehicles. "I do have a driver's license," he points out, "and I'm a much better driver than I was made out to be on the show. I loved the moment at the end of the year when I was with Clark and Chloe in the *Torch* office going over the information, and I offer to drive. They both went, 'No, that's all right — we'll take Chloe's car.' Little things like that were just for the fans, and I thought stuff like that was so cool."

Eric looks back fondly on the first season of *Smallville*. "It was such an education," he notes. "That was the greatest thing I took from the show, other than the friends that I made. I got an education on how to make a quality show, a show that people do care about, who want to do a really good job. I learned the little things that you cannot learn anywhere else except on set, and you only learn them after the crew is comfortable with you, and you are with them. They'd ask if I could do something a different way, to make their life easier. It was like college in eight months." ■

MARTHA KENT

"I didn't move to Smallville for action and glamour. I moved because a certain man told me we'd never be rich or travel the world, but he'd always love me. How could I pass up an offer like that?"

"**M**artha's one of those people who looks at the world the way I do," Annette O'Toole explains. "It's not that things are a joke, but that you can't take life too seriously or you'll go crazy. Especially if you're raising an alien son! I think it's good to go with the punches a little bit. She lives in a town that's very odd, and she's very intelligent. I think a lot of times she has to sit on her intelligence for whatever reason — sometimes just to keep the peace."

Annette wasn't the first person to play Martha Kent on *Smallville*. The highly experienced actress, who has appeared in numerous projects for film and television, including *Cat People* and *Stephen King's It*, was brought in to replace Cynthia Ettinger, who took the role in the unaired pilot. At the time that the opening episode was shot, Annette was committed to another series, *The Huntress*, but that was cancelled, leading to her suddenly becoming available. She had some initial reservations, because of the commitment to filming in Vancouver while her husband and family remained in Los Angeles, but once she saw the pilot, she was hooked, and agreed to meet with the executive producers.

"I think the producers felt they wanted someone older than Cynthia for the role, which I definitely am!" Annette laughs. "When we met, we were all on the same page with how we felt about the character and about the show. Since I'd seen the first version of the pilot, I wasn't going into it blind. Everybody else on the show had to guess that it was going to be good before they committed to it, but I didn't have to take everyone's word for it. I saw the final product, and it was just amazing — I got a couple of chills just watching it. In fact, I still get chills now because we're dealing with the legend of Superman, which has loomed so large in my life and in so many people's lives."

Part of the reason that Superman has been important to Annette stems from the fact that playing Martha Kent on the show doesn't mark Annette's first appearance in the sleepy town of Smallville. She appeared in the 1983 movie *Superman III* playing an older Lana Lang opposite Christopher Reeve, and at the time revealed that she had been a Superman fan since she was a child. "I used to trade the comics at school," she admits now. "I loved Superman for a few years, then I got more into the girly stuff. But I still have a comic book given to me by my first boyfriend, before he was my boyfriend and I just had a crush on him. We were appearing in *West Side Story* in Los Angeles — it was one of the *Jimmy Olsen* series, with Superman on the front, crying."

The actress has given serious thought to what Martha's life was like before the series opens, and has suggested ideas to Alfred Gough and Miles Millar which have been incorporated into Martha's onscreen background. "It's one of the things about this series

that I can relate to from my own life," she says. "I left Los Angeles and moved to Oregon for fourteen years, and raised my children there. I think Martha was a rich girl. She was from Metropolis. She found that it was all phony there, and she'd had enough of it. There was nobody that she could relate to on a real level. Her father wanted her to go in a certain direction, and I have the feeling that she didn't have a mother growing up — they've never introduced a mother for her. That's why being a mother is so important to her — and being the 'picture book' kind of mother at that. She found it very attractive to go with this wonderful man, Jonathan, into this new life, and totally embrace it. It's not that she can't go back, but it's just that it would be harder now."

The actress thinks that Martha is definitely sympathetic toward Lex. "He's the poor little rich boy," she says. "He's lost his mother, and he's lost his hair, which is traumatic for a kid at that age. And she knows what his father is like. She will always give him the benefit of the doubt. Even on the day when Lex goes completely to the dark side, Martha's still going to be saying, 'Oh, but remember, he just needs a hug!'"

She feels that making Lex Clark's boyhood friend is one of the best changes made for the series. "I think there's something so amazing about that," she notes, and adds that the fresh take on the legend that Gough and Millar devised "was the only way that could be done and made to work. You can't just keep telling the same story in the same way. The *Superman* movies, especially the first one, were just phenomenal, and they still really hold up well. I can't imagine a better Superman than Chris, so let's just stop there. But what was interesting to me, more than telling the teenage years story, was to tell the story that hasn't been told in a modern way. We are telling the story in terms of today and what kids have to deal with now. That was very appealing to me, and I liked the way that Clark's parents were going to be drawn into that as a real part of the formation of this young man, rather than not being seen at all. In a lot of television shows about teens, the parents are either not there or they're very ineffective, so it was nice to feel that the Kents were going to be pulled in and we'd see how they were going to be involved forming this guy."

She loves the ensemble cast. "I was looking around when I was on the set the other day," she says. "They're so lucky that they got all these people, because we really do love each other. There's nobody who we think, 'Oh God, here he comes again.' Everyone is so good. It's nice to be on a successful show that you can be proud of! I love feeling that I'm serving this show that I signed on to do, that I love, and this character whom I adore." ∎

JONATHAN KENT

"Your destiny may be to protect people, but ours is to protect you, and that's got to come first, OK?"

"Clark is not Superman in the making," John Schneider points out, "Clark is a special needs child." The father of three was attracted to *Smallville* because of the reality of the relationships between the teenagers and the adults, and it's something that he's fought to maintain throughout the series. "The thing that is important to me to keep going with Jonathan is that the least important person in Jonathan Kent's life is Jonathan Kent. I think that needs to be true of all dads, whoever and wherever they are. That should be the defining characteristic of a father."

Schneider is a veteran of the television industry, shooting to fame as Bo Duke on *The Dukes of Hazzard* and becoming a respected actor and director. Like many Hollywood professionals, he was aware of the pilot for *Smallville*, "and heard that it was another angle on the Superman legend," he recalls. "I was really uninterested, until I read the script. I thought it was really fantastic — it was an opportunity within a well-known device to bring back real parenting to television. There's been a lot of misrepresentation of the parental role on television, particularly the father, who has been depicted as the goof in the family. In *Smallville*, they represent the father as being part of the backbone of the family unit, and I think that's vitally important. One of the major problems that we have in society is that fathers aren't there. Parenting is a tag team operation. Jonathan and Martha don't always agree, but we always love one another, and we always do what's in the best interest of our son. *Smallville* isn't about the arrival of a hero, which is kind of what Superman was in his inception, but about the development of a hero. We are asking — and answering — the question, what made Clark Kent so good? That's exciting for me."

The actor is always pleased when the scripts reflect the reality of life on a farm for the Kents. "One of the things that grounded the show so much in reality," he maintains, "was that no matter what was going on with Clark, even when we were in our Freak of the Week stage, we still had bills to pay, we still had cows to milk, we still had equipment to fix — we still had a life. During the first season, we had the organic produce business. There was always something that we were doing that this new ability of Clark's would quite obviously be taking us away from. Annette and I are very aware of trying to keep a life obvious, outside of what's happening with Clark. Not that what is happening with Clark is not important, but I believe if the audience is aware that the crops are not going to get harvested because I love my son more than I love my responsibility to do that, then it actually strengthens the relationship. There has to be sacrifice. If we just have time to sit around the table, then that life can't be important to us. This is a working farm — there are things going on in order for these people to survive, and this special needs child's abilities are interrupting that life. If we lose that foundation of reality, then we

could become *Scooby-Doo*!

"If you go back to the pilot," he continues, "there was a great conversation between Clark and Jonathan after Lex gave him the truck, when he says it's not about the truck, it's not about Lex. 'I want you to know where the money came from that bought that truck.' Now that speaks volumes for the integrity of these people, the Kents."

Although the series may be centered around a teenager, Schneider is insistent that Jonathan and Clark "are not peers". He says firmly, "Once you start showing a forty-three-year-old and a sixteen-year-old as being peers rather than being parent and child, you completely blow the reality of the show. We may be the same height, but we are not peers. I do not look to him for approval. Otherwise it becomes Bo, Luke and Daisy Duke!"

Schneider admits that Jonathan Kent is often quick to anger, but that's not because he's a mean person. "I don't think he was short-tempered growing up," he says. "I think it comes from being protective. He's someone who feels that he knows the bad side of people. He's seen that bad side, and he wants to protect his family from that, even if it means he's got to be very strict. But I hope it's always clear that he loves his family."

Schneider feels that the conflict between Clark and Jonathan in 'Reaper' was well handled. "That was so real," he considers. "They were going fishing, and the work on the farm was put off. Jonathan had to get other people to take care of the farm, so he and Clark could have that time together. Because that had all been taken care of, and because Jonathan was so excited about it, and because they'd done it ever since Clark had come to Smallville, it made it so devastating when he said no. It was a family tradition."

Looking back at the first season, one of the scenes from 'Rogue' sums up Jonathan Kent for John Schneider. "He puts Phelan down in the coffee shop, and pretty much says, 'If you touch my son again, I'll kill you.' In that, you see the anger part of Jonathan Kent, but you also see that he's perfectly willing to go to jail, or worse, to protect his son."

"*Smallville* is a character-driven show," he concludes. "There are certainly some special effects in it, and the ones that we have are fantastic, but I'm glad that the producers don't make the mistake of leaning too heavily upon special effects, and foregoing the relationships. First and foremost, *Smallville* is a show about those relationships." ■

LIONEL LUTHOR

"If you're going to take me on, son, you're going to have to bring your game to a whole different level."

"I'm still working to make him human," John Glover says of the ruthless Lionel Luthor. "I don't want just to twirl my mustache!" Thanks to the color that the actor brings to the part, it's not likely that anyone is going to see the businessman as simply an uncomplicated villain.

Glover brings a wealth of experience to the role. Fans of the Caped Crusader will recognize his voice as that of Edward Nygma, aka the Riddler, in *Batman: The Animated Series*, while he perfected his devilish ways when he played Satan himself in the offbeat fantasy series *Brimstone*. During season one of *Smallville*, Glover combined his filming commitments on the show in Vancouver with stage work in New York, crossing the continent each week on his day off to become Lionel!

The actor revels in playing the shades of gray that are constantly being revealed in the elder Luthor. When he was approached initially for the role in the pilot, he was told that he would only be in a couple of scenes, but that the producers would be interested in him returning, depending on his schedule. "The potential for it looked interesting," Glover recalls, "but there was no need for me to make a commitment at that stage."

Like Chloe Sullivan, Lionel Luthor is entirely the creation of Alfred Gough and Miles Millar for the *Smallville* retelling of the Superman mythos, and Glover likes the clear canvas that this gives him to work on. Even at the very beginning, he could see nuances in the character. "He was just a businessman who seemed disappointed in his son," Glover says, "but that's quite a thing to play just there. He's a rich and powerful man, and his only son is a bit of a wuss and a bit of a fraidy-cat. The potential in that is enormous." One of the most powerful emotional scenes at the start of the pilot is Lionel's reaction to finding his suddenly bald son. "There was disgust and horror," Glover notes. "I think scenes like that are so popular because everybody interprets them in their own way."

From the first time that Lionel appeared in present-day Smallville, Glover aimed to show that he was trying to toughen Lex up. "What I was working on, and continue to work on, is to see him strengthen Lex," he says. "Lionel doesn't seem to be a man who wants his son to be afraid, so he's gone out of his way to give him tests, so he can prove himself. That's what locking him inside the plant in 'Jitters' was all about. Lionel makes the decision to close the gate. It's a tough decision, but he knows that if Lex survives, he will be a stronger person. No risk, no reward."

Glover is happy with the way Lionel is progressing. "There's a lot of *great* stuff I get to play," he says with relish. "The producers and writers are very collaborative, and they want to hear from us. They're not a dictatorship. They pay attention to what we're doing. I'm very lucky. It's juicy stuff they give Lionel!" ■

SHERIFF ETHAN

"You want to explain to me what a dead body's doing in your barn, Jonathan?"

"I first turned the part of the sheriff down because it was too small, just a few lines," Mitchell Kosterman recalls. "You have to make certain decisions about your career, and there's a certain size of role you're not going to take anymore. If you don't make that decision, you keep slipping backward. I had auditioned for a different part —someone's dad — and I was disappointed not to get it, because I wanted to be on the show. I wanted to be on something my kids could watch. I got a call and was offered the job as the sheriff, but I said no thanks. Then one of my agents got involved and said that it was going to be a recurring role. She said we ought not to walk away, because they've called twice, which is unusual. So she called them, and they said they were going to pay me significantly more than I'd ever made in my life!"

Mitchell's first filmed appearance was in 'Jitters', which had originally been designed to air third in the schedule, before reshoots pushed it back to the number eight slot. "I hardly spoke to anyone, said my couple of lines, and thought I'd never see it again," the actor admits. "A short time later, I was called back to do another episode and then another one. I think I did seven or eight in the first season. The first season I didn't have a lot to do acting-wise, until I had a couple of good scenes in 'Rogue', where my character developed to the point where it appeared I had a relationship with the Kent family, particularly Jonathan. We'd known each other for a long time. That's when I started to feel that I was part of the cast, and not just someone walking by in the background. For me, a big part of the joy of the experience is feeling like I'm part of the collaborative experience; that's what builds my self-esteem. That's what makes me happy."

A veteran of many shows filming in Vancouver, Mitchell has seen both ends of the spectrum in terms of on-set behavior, and notes that "*Smallville* seems to be unique. I never saw an actor have a tantrum. I never saw an actor verbally abuse another person — occasionally you'll see a property person abuse an extra because they haven't got their equipment on — not on *Smallville*. If you have good management and nice people at the top, the whole set seems to be that way." ■

MEET THE CREW

"The crew are here every single day, and they've got smiles, they've got jokes, they've got stories. Their attitude is so fantastic and it makes everyone's jobs easier. I love them!" — Kristin Kreuk

It takes literally hundreds of people to bring an episode of *Smallville* to life, from the writers, producers and support staff based at the series' Los Angeles offices, to the actors, crew, technical and support personnel at *Smallville*'s studios in Burnaby, British Columbia. Many members of the team have already been introduced in the course of the episode entries in this book, but this section focuses in more detail on the roles of some key players. It's no exaggeration to say that the show couldn't exist without all of them. Everyone has their part to play...

Bob Hargrove joined *Smallville* as the series' on-site producer at the start of the tenth episode. "I've started quite a few series," the veteran producer explains, "and I've never really found they get their legs until about the fifth or sixth episode. This one, unfortunately, was going through a lot more painful birth than others sometimes do. Miles and Al called me asking if I was available, and they brought me in to settle it down. Every production misstep will compute into dollars. My philosophy is that sometimes you have to spend dollars to deliver the product, and sometimes you have to spend dollars to get it to work. There were some hard choices, creatively, as well as for production, that had to be made in order to get it there."

Initially, the cast were working very long hours, and Hargrove "tried to bring normalcy to the production. I said that we weren't going to work sixteen hour days any more. We would work twelve hour days, and fit our schedules to make twelve hour days. There is a point of diminishing returns when you work sixteen hour days and six day weeks. You're totally wearing out your cast, and you're wearing out your crew."

Hargrove sees his job as helping the writers' dreams become reality. "We receive words, and those words have to be executed within the parameters of the studio sets," he explains. "For the majority of the time, we're able to do that. I don't think we've made any great sacrifices. We've been able to execute on an episode to episode basis more of what we wanted to do and made less sacrifices than on other shows I've done. Everybody stays calm, nobody yells, no one screams. You approach everybody with respect and dignity. There's no panic in this office. We just get it done. Everybody handles it that way, and I think that makes people happy. If you're happy to be here, then you're going to work harder, and it's not going to be as tough when you put in twelve or more hour days."

Opposite: The accident on Loeb Bridge from the Pilot — one of show's most memorable stunt sequences, reprised each week in the opening credits.

Smallville is a very challenging show for the production team. "The scripts are always very ambitious, and we have to get to a position where we can execute them without sacrificing a good product," Hargrove says. "A lot of series have one element that they deal with, but we deal with three different elements here. We deal with high drama,

which are our characters, and as far as I'm concerned they are what this show is about. People watch this show to watch Clark and Lana, Lex, Chloe, Pete, Lionel, Jonathan and Martha. They love these characters. That's all well and good, but we also have our action. We blow things up, we drop things — we create super hero moments which are sometimes difficult to achieve. And then we have our visual effects too.

"So we have these three elements that we have to put together — and we basically have eight days of principle photography and two days of second unit to do it. The biggest challenge on this show is to do that well, every week."

Rob Maier has been construction coordinator on *Smallville* right from the get-go, coming on board with the pilot. "I do more than what a usual construction coordinator does," he says. "My role here is certainly expanded greatly. I love the opportunity to do more than just my regular job. I do lots with the art department, assist with scheduling, and work closely with the producers. I'm in a real special place to be helpful in so many different areas. It's fantastic."

He is effectively in charge of the building work that is required for every episode of the show. "I don't think there's any other department that overlaps as much as we overlap," he continues. "We have to work in close concert with everyone in turn: the art department, the decorating department, the effects department, and props, and then after that grips, electric, and camera."

The art department and construction get the script very early in the process. "We've got an agreement with the producers that the quicker they can get the script to us, the quicker we can start reacting to it and also red-flagging it," he explains. "They feel exactly the same way. That makes a big difference to us. I attend all the meetings that I feel I should be at, and I'll go scouting with the producers every day, because for me it's helpful — I get to join in the creative process. They don't mind if I open my mouth, and I'm not a shy person. If I think something should be like this, then I say so, and if I get shot down, and my idea gets pooh-poohed, it could spur another idea. I can also help steer the art department or the director into or away from a path if I think it's not going to work because it'll take too much time."

Maier worked on "the entire five year run of *The X-Files* in Canada except for the pilot, and I was still standing at the end. That was good grooming for working on this. I was very reluctant to do another series, but I'm very happy and proud to be a part of this, and all of the folks that are here today are incredible people to work with and for. I was lucky enough to be involved with one major hit — to do two in a lifetime is pretty incredible. It doesn't happen very often."

Lauro Chartrand joined *Smallville* as stunt coordinator at the start of the filming of the regular episodes, beginning with 'Metamorphosis'. "I got involved through the first local producer up there in Vancouver," he explains. "I didn't have a lot of constraints — that was one of the nice things. It was pretty wide open. The bigger the better for the most part was the rule, which was pretty unusual for a TV show."

Although he is an experienced stuntman, Chartrand's role was primarily as coordinator. "I'm not a really good double for anyone they had on the show," he says. "Because it's a young show, the bad guys of the week were meant to be teenagers. I'm five-foot-six and 160 pounds, and the guys they had were five-foot-eleven and 140 pounds. I did however double for Whitney when he was crashing and rolling his trucks."

The truck roll in 'Metamorphosis' involved a cannon roll. "The effects guys build a cylinder in the passenger side of the vehicle, and usually put a chunk of telephone pole up in that cylinder with an explosive on top of it," Chartrand explains. "For this they used an air cannon, so they had a taller skinnier area to put the pole in, and then stuck a long rod in there. I got them to build a really good roll cage in the truck, then put in a driver's seat and a five point harness. I strap myself in, put on a helmet, and usually get going down the road at forty-five to fifty mph. You start to slide the truck ever so slightly in the direction you want it to roll, and you have a button that you hit that is charged with about 800 pounds of pressure, which pops the truck right over. At that speed, once you start rolling, you normally get three or four tumbles out of it."

Chartrand liked the opportunities that *Smallville* offered him. "They would write certain stunts into the scripts, but they would also let me dream up something I wanted to do, or something that hadn't been done before," he recalls. "I'd tell Greg Beeman that we'd never seen a truck go through a pane of glass as it's moving, so we did that for 'Leech'."

Below: Filming the truck roll in 'Metamorphosis'.

Above: The crew move in a for a close-up.

Caroline Cranstoun joined the series as costume designer for 'Hourglass', and continued to implement the design ideas that were started in the pilot. "The producers had a strong idea of what they wanted right away," she says. "We use a lot of color on the show."

Each character has their own designated color. "We started out by saying that Clark wears red, blue, and yellow, but we found that yellow wasn't something easy to incorporate," she points out. "He wears a lot of red, white, and blue, with touches of yellow, based on the Superman costume of course. His jackets are all either red, blue, or tan.

"Lana wears very pretty colors: pinks, blues, lavender, green. Pete wears bright colors — yellows and similar — and Chloe wears rich and bold colors, particularly purples. Jonathan wears greens and blues, mostly, and a lot of plaid. Martha wears very fall colors: rich ones like rusts, green, purples, and oranges. Lex wears strong colors: he's probably the only one of the cast who wears any black. He wears blacks, grays, blues, and purple, which is the Luthor color. Lionel is similar."

Cranstoun's responsibility covers all the background cast seen in any scenes in

Smallville High or the town. "The whole town is very colorful — whenever you see background, we try to make them as colorful as possible," she says. "Our set supervisor, Steve Oben, tries to dress the background like a gumball machine! It should look really colorful, and it usually does at the high school. There's a big distinction between anything that is Smallville and what we use for Metropolis. Smallville is friendly, happy, and bright — brown is as close to a black as we would use in Smallville. When we go to Metropolis, that's a different look. It's very urban, very New York. We don't really use brown there: black, grays, blues, reds, purples — strong, cold kinds of colors."

The department has a bit more leeway with regard to the guest stars. "Different ideas are tossed around," Cranstoun says. "We're not free to do anything, but we are open to do something a little different, and sometimes make them look a little bit bad or evil. We might use black or different colors, textures and styles we wouldn't use on someone else."

Cranstoun and her team don't usually have that much time to prepare the costumes. "Sometimes we have the luxury of a week," she says, "but sometimes it's a couple of days before filming. We get more notice on people who are coming up from LA than the local actors. You just have time to take their measurements and pull their costume together."

Executive producer **Ken Horton** takes charge of an episode in its closing stages. "After the shows are shot, there's an editor's cut, and then a director's cut," he explains. "At that point, they are doing the final draft of the show, and from then on, whatever you do is actually going to be seen by the audience. The largest part of my activity on the show starts there. I go in and huddle with the editor and director for about a day, and then I send a cut that goes to all the producers. They have notes, and then we proceed to finish the show. Al and Miles are very trusting of how I interpret their work. It has to fit a certain structure, regardless of what's written in the script, or how much has been shot. You have a teaser that you don't want to exceed four minutes. Four acts that have to be a minimum of six minutes and a maximum of eleven or twelve minutes. We shuffle scenes around from act to act, even occasionally from episode to episode."

To ensure he gets the material he needs, "we sit down with new directors before they go up to Canada. On an emotional and conceptual level, we say, 'Don't ever forget, no matter what this scene is about: Clark loves Lana, Lana loves Clark, Chloe loves Clark, Chloe likes Lana, Lana likes Chloe.' They could be talking about the weather, and when that scene is over, they're not talking about the weather. They are talking about some form of that existing emotion — otherwise they are just scenes."

Horton's aim is to keep the audience from thumbing the remote control and changing channel. "We read *Smallville* through color," he says. "It's interestingly different from other shows. It's vivid color presented basically in a 1950s approach. The framing of the shots is very simple: big heads with beautiful things around them. The close ups are highly decorated. The whole concept is of a teenage Eden where horrible things happen to everybody in every episode, yet there's a wish to find the place.

Above: Filming Clark's rescue of
Eric Summers in 'Leech'.

You want to live there. We don't mind if the visual effects are a little surreal, because the show is surreal. When we have cloud effects in a scene, they're moving. In real life, they don't do that, but we do that so the audience goes 'Wow!' It's just within the realm of any existing possibility."

Composer **Mark Snow** works with Ken Horton creating the musical underscore for the episodes. The various songs on the soundtrack are chosen by music supervisors Jennifer Pyken and Madonna Wade-Reed of Daisy Music, who select possibilities, which are discussed by the producers. Once a decision has been made, they then negotiate the rights.

Snow works from his home studio in Santa Monica. Summing the process up very quickly, he says: "I get a locked picture on a videotape which syncs up with all my gear in the studio. I write the music, finish it up, mix it up, send it through the airwaves on the internet, and the music editor puts it in. They call up usually and say, 'Thank you, well done.' Sometimes they call and say, 'Thank you, not so well done — can you change this or that?' I say 'Sure,' make the changes and send it back."

It's a lot more complicated than Snow makes it sound; he is bringing over twenty years of experience as a composer to *Smallville*, and it's a process of evolution. Snow will look at the picture and sit down at his keyboard to improvise — make the music up as he goes along — while he's watching. This is all being recorded, and he is then able to listen to it, and make changes so that he comes up with something that fits the scene — although not necessarily giving something in the music that goes exactly with every movement on screen.

"*Smallville* is a typical action-adventure orchestral romp," he says. "I think the uniqueness of the music is the contrast of that sound and seeing all these teenagers. It's a bit unexpected, but because of the sense of the mythology and the background of the Superman story, it seems to work. It's hard to imagine it now with a more electronic-sounding score with odd percussion and pulse. The producers seem to like the contrast of the modern songs and the traditional, orchestral approach to the score." ■

Below: How the rescue appeared onscreen.

THE PHENOMENON

"Like Clark, this baby's destined to fly." — *Newsday*

"*Smallville* was definitely a calculated fluke," says Peter Roth, President of Warner Bros. Television. "It was a carefully designed, clearly strategized, and as it turned out, well-crafted and well-produced series, and along with it being in the zeitgeist in the right place at the right time on the right network, that all conspired to success."

"The writing is intelligent, wittily playing off our knowledge of the Superman lore, and the production values are on a par with top quality fantasy/sci-fi shows like *The X-Files*. The WB's programmers hope *Smallville* will fill the void created by the defection of *Buffy the Vampire Slayer* to UPN. They shouldn't have to worry. *Smallville* is the most purely enjoyable dramatic series of the new season. Like Clark, this baby's destined to fly."

So wrote Noel Holston in *Newsday* magazine, previewing the début of the series on The WB. No words have ever been so prophetic. According to the *Hollywood Reporter*, one of the bibles of the show business industry, the pilot pulled in The WB's best-ever numbers. Around 8.35 million viewers tuned in to see the meteor shower hit *Smallville* and Clark Kent learning the truth about his past.

"The ability to take this American myth and reinterpret it for a younger audience that was discovering it for the first time, with many of the coming-of-age themes that dominate a lot of our programming, was a real victory for us," points out WB co-chief executive officer Jordan Levin. "It's become our most successful show. It has brought men to the network, while maintaining a very strong female audience. It probably was the first show for us that dads and their sons watched together — it has multi-generational appeal. It's a very broad-based appeal show, and a big hit."

Other news journals hailed the series' arrival, picking up on some of the key elements that would help the series continue to thrive. "Much of the interest in *Smallville* itself comes from the fact that the early signs of what lies in store for Clark are already becoming visible," the *National Review* pointed out. "The easy option (football stardom, in one episode) is not for him, and nor, it is understood, is the dark side. This Superman will be no Nietzschean lout... Except in the most literal sense, it is not Superman's powers that make him special, but what he chooses to do with them." *USA Today* noted that "there's talent and intelligence at work in *Smallville*", while the *Houston Chronicle* said that "this sly *Smallville* rises from the prequel cornfields to show surprising promise for that teen audience The WB loves so well... And *Smallville*'s charismatic star, Tom Welling, has the right stuff to be an overnight teen idol, even without flying around in a Superman suit." *Entertainment Weekly* hit the nail firmly on the head. "*Smallville*," it wrote, "seems capable of becoming an intriguing mix of teen angst and bright adventure."

While the show itself was going through some growing pains during the production of its early episodes, fans were flocking to the show. "I got the part and was doing some research on the internet, and there was already a site about it," Eric Johnson recalls, referring to KryptonSite, the Net's primary fan source of accurate factual information on the show. To find out more about the fictional world of *Smallville*, fans turned to the *Smallville Ledger* and *Torch* websites (excerpts from which appear alongside most episode entries in this book). These are under the control of Mark Warshaw (who contributed the story to 'Skinwalker' for the second season), working closely with the L.A. writers, the Vancouver production unit and a team of Warner Bros. International Television web writers and designers. Right from the very start, the site gave astute readers clues about upcoming episodes, with the names of future Freaks of the Week, such as Sean Kelvin, appearing in stories about their exploits before they took center stage in an episode. Fans who followed clues left on the site and in the show were even able to get a sneak preview of the future logos for LexCorp by 'monitoring' Lex's e-mails at the end of the season.

The series was quickly picked up around the world. A TV movie version of the first two episodes was broadcast in the United Kingdom on New Year's Eve 2001 on Channel 4, and the episodes were a great success. Unlike the majority of their American counterparts, British fans were able to see the series in widescreen versions right from the get-go.

During the first year, merchandise was basically confined to the DVD release of the TV movie of the pilot and 'Metamorphosis' in Canada in the summer of 2002, with numerous extras, including a commentary by Alfred Gough, Miles Millar, and for the pilot, David Nutter, which drops a few hints about the direction the show would take in its second year. Also included were an interactive map of Smallville and some deleted scenes. A full box set of the first season would eventually follow in September 2003, with crisp widescreen transfers of all the episodes. ■

Above: Clark, Lana and Lex ponder what the future holds in Season 2...

What I Learned This School Year

By Chloe Sullivan

Lesson 1: If it's weird, you must be in Smallville.

Lesson 2: High school is a constant state of metamorphosis. Just be careful what you change into.

Lesson 3: Allowing yourself to become a hothead will often cause you to burn bridges.

Lesson 4: If your friends need X-ray vision to discover your true inner self, you are suffering from an identity crisis.

Lesson 5: Kissing hot boys can be cool. Kissing hot boys to make yourself cool is not.

Lesson 6: Make the best of every stage of life, because you can never turn the hourglass over.

Lesson 7: If you have a craving for roadkill, you need to see a physician immediately...

Lesson 8: If you have excessive jitters, you need to see a physician immediately.

Lesson 9: Nothing good ever comes from being a rogue.

Lesson 10: A shimmer of jealousy can turn to obsession.

Lesson 11: Friends hug. Lovers kiss. And if you're gonna kiss, it's always good to have something minty beforehand.

Lesson 12: If you're gonna leech off others greater than you, then be careful, because with great power comes great responsibility. (Don't ask me where I've heard that one before.)

Lesson 13: When encountering people with way too much kinetic energy, stay away from third-story windows.

Lesson 14: There is no such concept as 'zero consequences'.

Lesson 15: Over 100 years ago, Nicodemus flowers nearly killed off half the state of Kansas before becoming extinct. If you come into contact with one, beware: harmful side effects include running people off the road, pointing guns at friends and family members, displaying inappropriate public affection, climbing windmills, and taking off your clothes in the middle of school.

Lesson 16: If you encounter anyone claiming to read your mind, be extra careful where you allow your thoughts to stray.

Lesson 17: There is very good justification for why the grim reaper has long been the symbol of death.

Lesson 18: Drones do not good leaders make.

Lesson 19: A crush is just a crush. Love is something totally different.

Lesson 20: Once you've been kidnapped, your life becomes like a personal camera obscura — things seem to get flipped.

Lesson 21: No matter how large the tempest, there is nothing that can't be overcome when you have good friends and family to count on.